Bertil Lintner

THE RISE AND FALL OF THE COMMUNIST PARTY OF BURMA (CPB)

Bertil Lintner

THE RISE AND FALL OF THE COMMUNIST PARTY OF BURMA (CPB)

Southeast Asia Program
120 Uris Hall
Cornell University, Ithaca, New York
1990

Maps prepared by David K. Wyatt

CPB leaders at the 30th Anniversary, Panghsang, March 28, 1979.
Left to right, Tin Yee, Myo Myint, Thakin Pe Tint, Thakin Ba Thein Tin.
Photo: CPB Archives

CONTENTS

Illustrations

MAPS

Opium for sale in Panghsang market. Photo: Hseng Noung Lintner.

Panghsang market. Photo: Hseng Noung Lintner.

INTRODUCTION

One of Asia's longest Communist insurrections ended on the night of April 16, 1989. Its cessation was not the outcome of a successful government offensive or of a generous amnesty policy, but of an all-out mutiny within the rank-and-file of the insurgent Communist Party of Burma (CPB). That night, mutineers stormed the CPB's headquarters at Panghsang, near the Chinese frontier in Burma's northeastern Shan State. The rebellious troops seized the well-stocked central armory and other buildings. While they were smashing portraits of Communist icons Marx, Engels, Lenin, Stalin, and Mao Zedong and destroying CPB literature in an outburst of anti-party feeling, the CPB's aging, staunchly Maoist leadership fled headlong across the Nam Hka border river to China. For the first time in history, a Communist insurgency had been defeated from within its own ranks.

The tumultuous event at Panghsang on April 16–17 came after years of simmering discontent with the old leadership which had stubbornly refused to give up an increasingly anachronistic political line, unchanged since the days of the Cultural Revolution in China of the late 1960s. Perhaps more importantly, the mutiny reflected ethnic tensions within the party. The overwhelming majority of the CPB rank-and-file comes from various minority peoples in the Sino-Burmese border mountains, and these have always been motivated by ethnicity and general anti-government sentiments rather than ideology. Nearly all of the CPB's military commanders were also from these ethnic groups—Wa, Kokang Chinese, Kachin, Shan, and others—with aging, Burman Marxist-Leninists only as party leaders and as political commissars attached to the various units.

Another important factor behind the mutiny was the lucrative drug trade in the CPB's base area. During the CPB's third—and last—party congress held in 1985, it was decided to take stern measures against opium trading, the manufacture of heroin, and other "illegal activities" in which local cadres had become involved. Party agents were sent to check up on local cadres and report any wrongdoing to the center. This writer noted in 1987: "If strictly enforced, the policy could create serious conflicts between the CPB's ideologically motivated top leadership and the party's many local cadres who are benefitting from the drug trade. This puts the whole feasibility of the [anti-drug] campaign into question, and most local observers believe it likely that the campaign will eventually be abandoned to prevent a split in the party."[1] The campaign was not abandoned and the inevitable happened.

---

[1] *Far Eastern Economic Review,* June 4, 1987.

Seen in a broader perspective, the events that eventually led to the demise of the CPB were an outcome of changing power patterns in the region, in particular the new foreign policy adopted by China after the death of Mao Zedong in 1976. The resultant, severe cut-back in Chinese aid to the Communist insurgencies in the region contributed to the almost immediate collapse of the Communist Party of Thailand (CPT) and the final demise of the Communist Party of Malaya (CPM). In Burma, however, the Communist insurrection continued—although the reduction in Chinese aid severely affected the CPB's ability to equip its troops and to maintain schools and hospitals in the territory under its control. This forced the CPB to introduce heavy and unpopular taxes on the population under its control, further alienating the leadership from the local people in the northeastern base area.

The fact that the CPB—unlike the CPT and the CPM—remained a potent insurgent force until 1989 reflected the uncompromising stand of the government it was opposing. The military régime in Rangoon has persistently refused to seek a political solution to Burma's civil war and has, in fact, used the existence of a civil war and a "Communist threat" to justify the army's dominant role in Burmese politics. Some observers have, therefore, suspected that the country's military rulers never were—and are still not—interested in finding a permanent solution to the problem.

Since seizing power in 1962, the military rulers of Burma have never offered a tolerant amnesty program, as did Thailand, for example, under order 66/2532 by former Prime Minister Prem Tinsulanonda. Nor has the Burmese military ever tried to implement either a "winning-the-hearts-and-minds-policy" or any other element of Sir Robert Thompson's concept of counter-insurgency through psychological warfare, which characterized the British campaign against the Communist insurrection in Malaya in the 1950s. On the contrary, Rangoon has always demanded unconditional surrender from all rebels in the country—even during the peace talks of 1963 and the "general amnesty" of 1980. The current rulers of the State Law and Order Restoration Council (SLORC) retain the same inflexible attitude which was demonstrated on May 25, 1989, when Col. Aung Thein, a SLORC spokesman, turned down a Thai offer to mediate in Burma's civil war, saying: "We shall fight the insurgents until they are eliminated."

A BRIEF HISTORY OF THE CPB
1939–1968

The CPB was founded on August 15, 1939 when a group of young Burmese intellectuals met in a small flat in Barr Street, Rangoon. Among them were several student leaders from the Dohbama Asiayone or "Our Burma Association," the most militant nationalist political party in Burma before World War II: Thakin Aung San, Thakin Thein Pe, Thakin Ba Hein, and Thakin Hla Pe, later known as Bo Let Ya. The charismatic Aung San was elected general secretary and in official party history this unpretentious meeting in Rangoon is called the CPB's First Party Congress.[1]

The decades that preceded the formation of the CPB were some of the most turbulent in modern Burmese history. In December 1920, a large body of students—who have always been at the forefront of any political movement in Burma—launched a strike to protest a new university act which would have transformed Rangoon University into an élite institution designed to produce a narrow stratum of qualified Burmese who could take over the jobs done by foreigners. This proposal, the students claimed, had been made without consulting the Burmese public. The students camped at the foot of the gold-covered Shwe Dagon Pagoda, Burma's holiest shrine, to press their demands against the British authorities, and the strike spread to colleges and even high schools throughout Burma proper. The authorities gave in to some of the student demands and the anti-colonial struggle gained momentum.

In 1930 a peasant revolt, led by Saya San, broke out in Yetaik village in Tharrawaddy district, from where it spread throughout southern Burma. Saya San's followers styled themselves *galons* after the garuda, a powerful bird in Hindu

---

[1]According to Bo Let Ya, apart from himself, Thakins Thein Pe, Ba Hein, and Aung San, an unnamed "friend from Calcutta" participated in this meeting (Bo Let Ya, "Snapshots of Aung San" in *Aung San of Burma*, ed. Maung Maung [The Hague: Martinus Nijhoff, 1962]). According to Ba Thein Tin (interview, Panghsang, December 23, 1986), Thakin Aung San, Thakin Hla Pe (Bo Let Ya), Thakin Ba Hein, Thakin Bo, Dr Nag, and H. N. Goshal were present at the "1st Congress." Ba Thein Tin also says that Thakins Soe and Than Tun did not participate in this meeting but joined the party shortly afterwards. According to Thein Pe Myint ("Critique of the Communist Movement in Burma," dated 1973, in *Documents on Communism in Burma 1945–77*, ed. Klaus Fleischmann [Hamburg: Mitteilungen des Instituts für Asienkunde, 1989]), Burma's first Communist cell included Thakin Aung San, Thakin Soe, Thakin Ba Hein, Thakin Hla Pe (Bo Let Ya), and H. N. Goshal. Thein Pe Myint also states that he himself initiated this meeting but "was left out from the first party cell for his individualism and sectarianism on the part of some comrades," and that Thakin Than Tun was "not Communist enough to be in the first cell."

mythology—and believed that their tattooes and amulets would make them invulnerable to British bullets. Although the rebellion was eventually crushed, in a psychological sense it helped pave the way for the eventual success of Burma's independence movement. Saya San was the traditional *minlaung* (pretender) to the old Burmese throne, a figure often produced in times of crisis. He wanted a return to the world of the old Buddhist kingdom of pre-British days, but the young nationalists did not miss the point that most of his followers were young monks and impoverished farmers, and the rebellion had clearly demonstrated their potential.

Radical social ideas had already entered Burma from India and Britain, and the royalties from a book written by Saya San funded the establishment of a library of the first Marxist literature to reach Burma. Most of this literature was brought in by students returning from England, and a number of book clubs—notably the *Nagani* ("Red Dragon") Book Club—were set up in Rangoon and elsewhere. From then onwards, socialist ideas influenced nearly every political organization in Burma, including the powerful Dohbama Asiayone and the prestigious Rangoon University Students' Union (RUSU). The militant young nationalists called themselves *thakins* or "masters," a title hitherto used for the British. By adding this title to their names, they intended to show that they, the Burmese, were the real masters of the country.

A second student strike occurred in 1936 when the RUSU president, Thakin Nu (later U Nu) and his close associate Thakin Aung San were expelled from the campus. The two were eventually re-instated, but by that time the movement had taken an even more definite anti-colonial stand. The anti-British movement, no longer confined to the activities of groups of militant students in Rangoon, spread across the country in the 1930s. The peasants, hard-hit by the collapse of the international rice market in 1930 and burdened by heavy taxes, were rapidly losing their land to money-lenders and absentee landlords. By the end of the decade, Burma was ripe for a nationwide uprising.

Two years after the second student strike at Rangoon University, the young nationalists spearheaded a mass uprising, and 1938 became known as "The Year of the Revolution," or "The 1300 Movement," since, according to the Burmese calendar, it was the year 1300. A strike broke out among militant workers in the Yenangyaung oil fields southwest of Mandalay. In Rangoon, the students took to the streets and demonstrated against the British authorities. When the police charged the demonstrators a young student, Aung Gyaw, suffered a bad head wound from a baton blow, and died in hospital shortly afterwards. He was immediately proclaimed a martyr and all over the country the incensed public joined in the protests.[2] In Mandalay, on February 15, 1939, the police opened fire on a huge demonstration, killing seventeen people of whom seven were Buddhist monks. "Out of this national and class struggle of the Burmese people and working class emerges the Communist Party of Burma," the CPB declared much later in its official party history.[3]

---

[2]For a detailed account of those events, see Khin Yi, *The Dobama Movement in Burma (1930–1938)* (Ithaca: Cornell University Southeast Asia Program, 1988).

[3]*A Short Outline of the History of the Communist Party of Burma:* official party document dated June 1964, and printed in Beijing.

According to British documents, the "father of Burmese communism" was Oo Kyaw, the son of a big landowner in Henzada district.[4] After passing high school finals in Burma and the London Matriculation in Ceylon, he went to London in 1927 to study for the Bar. Already strongly influenced by Bengali revolutionaries and by the India-based League Against Imperialism, he traveled widely in Europe where he contacted various Communist groups. Oo Kyaw was believed to have been instrumental in sending Marxist literature back to Burma, and through a lively correspondence with a few selected student leaders back home in Rangoon he managed to pull the movement against the British sharply towards the left.

Quite independently from the emergence of an Indian- and British-inspired radical student movement among the Burman intellectuals, Communist ideas had also penetrated Rangoon's Chinese community in the late 1920s. "Chinese communism" was first introduced into Burma by Wu Wei Sai (alias Wu Ching Sin) and his wife who arrived in Rangoon in May 1929 from Shanghai. Wu became editor-in-chief of a Chinese-language daily newspaper called *Burma News*, while his wife became a teacher at the Chinese-medium Peng Min School in Rangoon. The couple distributed Communist leaflets in Rangoon's Chinatown and built up a small circle of followers. Their activities were discovered in December 1929 when the British police Special Branch intercepted a letter Wu Wei Sai had written in invisible ink to the South Seas Communist Party in Singapore.[5]

His main message appears to have been that there was no fertile ground for Communist ideas among the largely business-oriented Chinese community in Burma. Unlike Singapore and Malaya, Burma had very few laborers of Chinese origin: almost all coolies, dockworkers, and other manual laborers in Rangoon were Indian. Wu Wei Sai therefore left Burma in 1930 and was never heard of again. Only half-a-dozen members remained in a cell with the pretentious name "the Provisional Committee of the Special Division, Burma, Branch of the South Seas Communist Party." Because they were Chinese, the British police were able to have some of them deported to China. A Chinese cell was also established in Pyinmana but neither this group nor the underground Communist movement in Rangoon's Chinatown had any contacts with the radical Burman movement; instead, their links were with the Chinese-dominated Communist parties in Malaya and Singapore.

As far as it is known, the Burman nationalists were unaware of the existence of these Chinese cells. Had the two groups established contact in the late 1930s, it is possible that communism might even have succeeded in Burma. For, despite their Indian connections, the young Burmese radicals pinned their hopes for help in their struggle against the British on Mao Zedong and his Communist army in China, but did not know how to contact them. The *thakins* met in Rangoon in 1940, and decided to send Aung San to Shanghai, where they knew the Chinese Communists were strong. Eager to elude the British police, Aung San took the first ship to China he could find in Rangoon port: it was destined for Amoy, then occupied by the Japanese. He was taken to Tokyo; in the following year, he returned to Rangoon to fetch more of the young *thakins* for military training in Japan. They arrived in batches, smug-

---

[4]Express Letter from the Chief Secretary to the Govt. of Burma, Police Department, No 173-C-34, dated March 17, 1934. Reproduced in *Communism in India—Unpublished Documents 1925–1934* (Calcutta: National Book Agency, 1980), p. 170.

[5]Ibid. pp. 177–78. The document does not give the Chinese name for the newspaper. It ceased publication in November 1929.

gled out on Japanese freighters from Rangoon. When the complete band had assembled, and been joined by one Burmese who was studying drama in Tokyo, they added up to thirty dedicated young men. Consequently, they became known as "The Thirty Comrades."

However, the connection with Japan was not established simply because Aung San caught the wrong ship in Rangoon in 1940. Japan's secret activities in Burma were undertaken by various agents in Rangoon and elsewhere. In the 1930s a Japanese naval officer called Shozo Kokubu had made contact with a faction of the Dohbama Asiayone led by Thakin Tun Oke and Ba Sein. In 1940 another Burmese nationalist, Dr. Thein Aung, had visited Tokyo on a trip arranged by a Japanese agent in Rangoon, Dr Tsukasa Suzuki.[6] Other left-leaning *thakins*, led by Thakin Kodaw Hmaing and including Aung San, were suspicious of the Japanese, and the aborted trip to China should be seen as an attempt to find another source of support for the struggle for independence. When that failed, only the Japanese option was open to the young Burmese nationalists.

By now it was clear that the initial unity among the *thakins* belonged to the past. Previously there had been an abundance of different political parties: the main Dohbama, the CPB, the closely associated People's Revolutionary Party (PRP), the Sinyetha or "Poor Man's Party," and others. But these names had meant little, since the activities and even the policies of these parties generally overlapped, and since many people were members of two or three parties at the same time. Now, however, various rival factions began to emerge—and the main division of opinion was between the left-leaning Thakin Kodaw Hmaing faction of the Dohbama and the Thirty Comrades on the one hand, and on the other the more Axis-oriented Ba Sein-Tun Oke group. Aung San, Bo Let Ya, and the more prominent of the *thakins* belonged to the former faction while Ne Win—one of the Thirty Comrades who later was to become Burma's military dictator—was one of the most prominent members of the latter.[7]

After spending some months in Tokyo and on the Japanese-held islands of Hainan and Formosa, the Thirty Comrades were transferred to Bangkok, Thailand, where the Burma Independence Army (BIA) was set up on December 26, 1941. When they entered Burma, thousands of young Burmese nationalists joined the BIA. Serving alongside the Japanese army, they participated in the capture of Rangoon on March 7, 1942 while the British retreated north and eventually evacuated all their forces to India. On August 1, 1943, the Japanese granted "independence" to Burma. Dr Ba Maw, who had led the Sinyetha in the late 1930s became *adipadi*, or Head of State. Aung San had all along been the military leader of the Burmese nationalist forces which, however, operated strictly under Japanese command.

Aung San and several of the initial founders of the CPB had drifted away from the party; they were basically nationalists influenced by Marxist ideas rather than hardcore Communists. But some of the Burmese intellectuals were still upholding the banner of the CPB, and they gradually emerged as a distinct political grouping. Among them were Thakin Soe, a fiery young radical who had participated in "The 1300 Movement"; H.N. Goshal alias Thakin Ba Tin, a Burmese of

---

[6]Won. Z. Yoon, "Japan's Scheme for the Liberation of Burma: The Role of the Minami Kikan and the Thirty Comrades," unpublished paper from Ohio University Center for International Studies, 1973, pp. 7–9.

[7]Interview with Bo Kyaw Zaw, one of the Thirty Comrades, Panghsang, January 1, 1987.

Bengali origin; Dr. Nag alias Tun Maung, another Bengali revolutionary who had lived in Burma for a long time; Thakin Ba Hein, a student leader and a theoretician who actually built up the CPB; Thakin Than Tun, a school teacher from Pyinmana who had joined the party shortly after "the 1st Congress" in 1939 (he was Aung San's brother-in-law); Thakin Ba Thein Tin, a Sino-Burman from Tavoy; and Thakin Thein Pe, a veteran of the Dohbama Asiayone and the student movement in Rangoon.

The official party history distinguishes between three different periods in the early days of the party, prior to the outbreak of civil war in 1948:

1939–1941: "From the day of its inception, the CPB launched an active anti-British struggle up till 1941."[8]

This overstatement basically meant that the Burmese Communists were active in the Dohbama Asiayone and other nationalist groups, including Dr. Ba Maw's Sinyetha party and the Freedom Bloc, which he set up in October 1939. No party records have been preserved from this period, and the work with the by far more important Dohbama claimed most of their time anyway. In early 1940, the same group of Communists and non-Communist radicals set up the PRP which was led by Thakin Aung San, Thakin Mya, Thakin Ba Hein, Thakin Hla Pe (Bo Let Ya), Thakin Chit, Thakin Nu (U Nu), Thakin Kyaw Nyein, Ba Swe, Thakin Hla Maung (Bo Zeya), and Thakin Thun Shwe or, in other words, the most prominent student radicals of the time. The PRP was a parallel organization to the CPB and far more important at this stage. Thakin Ba Hein acted as liaison officer between the PRP and the CPB, which was beginning to take shape as a separate political party under the leadership of Thakin Than Tun, Thakin Soe, H. N. Goshal, and others. But in reality it was still too early to talk about a properly organized Communist party in Burma.

1941–1945: "After the Hitlerites treacherously attacked the Soviet Union, the CPB changed its tactics and directed its blows against the fascists . . . the CPB worked untiringly to oppose the Japanese fascists and actively prepared for armed struggle against the Japanese fascists. In 1944, under the leadership of the CPB, the Anti-Fascist People's Freedom League (AFPFL) was formed . . . on 27 March 1945, the Burmese people under the leadership of the CPB started their glorious armed struggle against the Japanese fascists in Burma."[9]

This is a rather liberal interpretation of the fact that the loosely organized Burmese Communists were, ironically, the first to contact the Western Allies at a time when Aung San and the non-Communists were still siding with the Japanese, as in British Malaya where the Communists also cooperated with the colonial power against the Japanese.

---

[8]*A Short Outline*, p. 1.

[9]Ibid., pp. 1–2.

Already in July 1941, writing from Insein Jail, Thakin Than Tun and Thakin Soe issued a document known as "the Insein Manifesto,"[10] in which they favored a temporary alliance with the British in face of the danger of a Japanese attack against Burma—which actually did take place in December of that year. In July 1942, after the Japanese invasion, two Communists, Thakin Thein Pe and Thakin Tin Shwe, reached Calcutta where they were introduced to Force 136, the arm of the Special Operations Executive (SOE) established to work behind Japanese lines in Southeast Asia. Secret contacts were made with the nationalists who were becoming increasingly disappointed with the Japanese. On March 27, 1945, the Burma National Army (BNA—which had succeeded the Burma Defence Army in 1943 which, in turn, had succeeded the BIA in 1942) declared war on the Japanese. Just before the uprising, the BNA was 11,480 strong and was supported by the British.[11] For strategic purposes, the country was divided into eight military regions:

No 1 Region (Prome, Henzada, Tharrawaddy, and Insein). Military commander: Aung San; Political adviser: Thakin Ba Hein;
No 2 Region (Pyapon/Eastern Irrawaddy delta). Military commander: Ne Win (one of the Thirty Comrades); Political adviser: Thakin Soe;
No 3 Region (Western Irrawaddy delta). Military commander: Saw Kya Doe (a Karen);
No 4 Region (South of Toungoo/Hanthawaddy). Military commander: Kyaw Zaw (one of the Thirty Comrades); Political adviser: Thakin Chit (PRP leader);
No 5 Region: (Tavoy-Mergui). Military commander: Tin Tun; Political adviser: Thakin Ba Thein Tin (prominent CPB member);
No 6 Region (Pyinmana-Meiktila). Military commander: Bo Ye Htut (one of the Thirty Comrades); Political adviser: Thakin Kyaw Nyein (ex-student leader);
No 7 Region (Thayetmyo-Minbu). Military commander: Bohmu Aung (one of the Thirty Comrades); Political adviser: Thakin Tin Mya (CPB member);
No 8 Region (Upper Burma). Commander: Bo Ba Htoo.

The set-up reflected the close relationship which now existed between the Communists and the non-Communist nationalists—although it would have been a clear exaggeration to say that it was the CPB that actually led the struggle. The AFPFL was a front, comprising nationalists as well as Communists and even some regional groupings. Aung San, Ne Win, and Bo Let Ya represented the army; Thakin Soe, Thakin Than Tun, and Thakin Tin Mya came from the CPB; and Thakin Ba Swe, Thakin Kyaw Nyein, and Thakin Chit were from the PRP. On May 1, 1945, Rangoon was liberated, and the last Japanese forces withdrew from Burma a few months later.

The CPB was now at the height of its strength and popularity because of the crucial role the Communists unquestionably had played in the anti-Japanese struggle. According to rough estimates, 30,000 guerrillas were controlled by the CPB and,

---

[10]Jan Becka, *The National Liberation Movement in Burma during the Japanese Occupation Period* (Prague: The Oriental Institute in Academia, Publishing House of the Czechoslovak Academy of Sciences, 1983), p. 53.

[11]Ibid., p. 223.

according to one source, these troops were responsible for about 60 percent of all the casualties which were inflicted on the Japanese.[12] The BNA was renamed the Burma Patriotic Forces and was recognized by Louis Mountbatten as "an allied force" at a meeting in New Delhi on May 30.

During this period, the CPB developed into a true political party, not just a Marxist study group comprising people who spent most of their time working for other parties, as had been the case in 1939–1941. In early 1943, Thakin Soe gave a course to twelve followers in the delta town of Pyapon; this event is seen by many scholars as the real origin of the CPB.[13] In January 1944, another meeting was held in Nyaungkyuang village of Kyaiklat township; it was attended by seven people, including Thakin Soe and Thakin Tin Mya. Thakin Soe was elected secretary general of the CPB. This meeting is sometimes referred to as the CPB's Second Congress, but it was not recognized by the main party.[14] At this time, however, many prominent Burmese became party members, either temporarily because of the relative popularity of the CPB, or permanently as dedicated Communists. Ne Win belonged to the former group;[15] Bo Ye Htut, Bo Zeya, and a few other heroes of the anti-Japanese struggle belonged to the latter.

1945–1948: "In May, 1945, the CPB for the first time could work as an open, legal party. The CPB directed its main blow against the British imperialists who had once again become the rulers of Burma. . . . In August 1946, the CPB led the greatest general strike in the postwar period. . . . From May 1945 up till March 1948, the CPB led various strikes of the workers' and peasants' movement in the countryside. During this period almost all the trade union organizations in Burma were organized by the CPB. The CPB also organized peasants' unions whose paid-up membership reached a total of nearly one million."[16]

The efficiency of the CPB's organization increased notably during this period. The party was reorganized into an effective Communist organization at the Second Party Congress, which was held on July 20–21, 1945 in Rangoon. It was attended by more than 120 delegates from all over the country, representing a total of 6,000 party members (not including members of CPB-affiliated mass organizations). A 21-member Central Committee was elected; it named Thakin Than Tun chairman of the Politbureau, and Thakin Thein Pe new general secretary—in absentia since he was still in India. Thakin Thein Pe returned to Burma later that year and assumed leadership of the party. The CPB at this time advocated a peaceful transition to socialism, a line which later was branded "Browderism" after the reformist doctrines of the then chairman of the Communist Party of the United States, Earl Browder.

An extended plenum of the CPB was held in February–March 1946. Thakin Soe, a hardliner who felt his wartime role in the underground entitled him to greater recognition, launched a sharp attack on the party leadership. He seized upon the issue of "Browderism," and submitted a memorandum, accusing Thakin Than Tun

[12]Interview with Bo Kyaw Zaw, Panghsang, January 1, 1987.

[13]Becka, *National Liberation Movement*, p. 145.

[14]Interview with Thakin Ba Thein Tin, Panghsang, December 23, 1986.

[15]Becka, *National Liberation Movement*, p. 170.

[16]*A Short Outline*, p. 2.

and Thakin Thein Pe of advocating the moderate line. In retaliation, Thakin Than Tun accused Thakin Soe of immorality and "sexual misconduct." Thakin Soe succeeded in forcing his two rivals to step down temporarily. During the leadership vacuum, Soe tried to fill the Central Committee with his own people—but this backfired when Thakin Than Tun and Thakin Thein Pe returned to power after a few days.[17]

The break between Thakin Soe and the main party was now final and irrevocable; he set up his own Communist Party (Red Flag) and went underground in the Irrawaddy Delta to wage a guerrilla war against the British. Some of the other hardline Communists, including Thakin Tin Mya and six members of the Central Committee, sided with Thakin Soe in the conflict. The Burmese government later described Thakin Soe in these terms: "He reads voraciously and writes profusely. He is extremely ruthless in his methods and combines in himself the qualities of a terrorist, a voluminous pamphleteer and a dauntless campaigner.... He has a considerable following ... in Maubin, Pyapon and Hanthawaddy districts and ... in Pakokku and Lower Chindwin districts."[18]

The question of "Browderism" became more controversial after a meeting between Lord Mountbatten and the Burmese wartime resistance leaders in Kandy in September 1945. Then it was decided to dismantle the large army Aung San and others had built up, and to form a new Burmese Army consisting of a mere 4,700 troops. But about 3,500 ex-resistance fighters did not register for regular enlistment and instead formed the Pyithu Yebaw Ahphwe (ပြည်သူ့ ရဲတော် အဖွဲ့.), which became known in English as the People's Volunteer Organization (PVO). In effect, it was a paramilitary force controlled by Aung San. Nonetheless, the Kandy Agreement was seen by the hardline Communists as a surrender to the British. At this time, Thakin Than Tun argued that the idea of launching open warfare against the British was "unrealistic" and "politically wrong"; he also claimed that the US-UK-Soviet conferences at Teheran, Yalta, and Potsdam had laid solid foundations for the peaceful cooperation of all nations within the framework of the United Nations. Given the strong position of the Soviet Union and "the socialist forces" all over the world, armed struggle against "the imperialists" was not necessary.[19]

Despite this "right-wing opportunism"—as the hardliners described the official policies of the CPB—the gap between the party and the non-Communist nationalists was widening steadily. The CPB had joined Aung San's pre-independence cabinet and Thakin Thein Pe had even been appointed minister for forest and agriculture, then the highest position held by a Communist in the British Empire. It was at this point that the CPB, in August 1946, launched "the greatest general strike in the post-war period"—which independent historians would describe as a minor rising in Yamethin and Toungoo districts. The CPB also began attacking Aung San personally, accusing him of "betraying the nationalist cause" by participating in the British-initiated pre-independence government—despite the fact that Thakin Thein Pe was also included in that cabinet. It is hardly surprising that the CPB was expelled from the AFPFL in October (1946), or that Thakin Thein Pe was

---

[17]Charles B. McLane, *Soviet Strategies in Southeast Asia* (Princeton, NJ: Princeton University Press, 1966), pp. 326–27.

[18]*Burma and the Insurrections* (Rangoon: Government of Burma publications, September 1949), p. 3.

[19]Becka, *National Liberation Movement*, p. 258.

forced to resign from his post after less than three weeks in office. He subsequently drifted away from the CPB as well, until he left the party entirely just before the armed uprising broke out in March 1948. Thakin Than Tun had resigned as AFLFP general secretary in July 1946; after the expulsion of the CPB from the front he was succeeded by the acting secretary general, Kyaw Nyein. Subsequent attempts to reunify the CPB and the AFPFL failed.[20]

The CPB, however, had managed to penetrate Burma's fledgling trade union movement. On June 1, 1945, the All-Burma Trade Union Congress (ABTUC) had been set up in Rangoon with a prominent Communist, Thakin Ba Hein, as its first leader. Altogether fourteen trade unions, with a total membership of 11,150 workers, were then affiliated to the ABTUC. On July 9 it applied for membership in the World Federation of Trade Unions. The All-Burma Peasants' Union (ABPU) was another organization which the Communists had managed to infiltrate. Under the guise of the ABPU, the Communists mobilized the peasants in "no rent, no taxes" campaigns. They even confiscated land from big landlords and distributed it to the cultivators, which earned them a certain degree of popularity in the countryside. In Rangoon, the CPB published its own daily newspaper, *Kommyunit Nezin* (ကွန်မြူနစ် နေ့စဉ်; "Communist Daily"), as well as a weekly theoretical journal, *Pyithu Ana* (ပြည်သူ့ အာဏာ; "People's Power"). However, it should also be stressed that the Communists were less successful than the PRP (which in August 1945 had become the Burma Socialist Party, the BSP) in recruiting a mass following. The BSP had chosen to work within the AFPFL and strengthen it, which made that party more popular than the CPB among Burma's many socialists.

The CPB's shift from a legal opposition party to an underground insurgent organization began in April 1947 when it carried out a half-hearted boycott of the elections to the new Constituent Assembly. Although the CPB did not participate as an organization, it fielded twenty-eight candidates, of whom only seven were elected to the 255-member assembly: the juggernaut AFPFL captured the remaining 248 seats. The CPB's reluctance to participate in the parliamentary process may have been prompted by the realization that the party would not stand a chance against the AFPFL in free and fair elections. Instead, the party continued to work within the "mass organizations" in order to build up a power base, especially among Burma's peasants and workers.

The "peaceful line" was gradually being given up as the CPB increased its contacts with the international Communist movement. In 1947, Thakin Ba Thein Tin— a member of the Politbureau since 1946—and *yebaw* Aung Gyi represented the CPB at the British Empire Communist Conference in London. More importantly, a six-man CPB delegation went to Calcutta in February 1948 to attend the second congress of the Communist Party of India (CPI). The group consisted of Thakin Than Tun, Thakin Ba Thein Tin, *yebaw* Aung Gyi, Bo Yan Aung (one of the Thirty Comrades who had joined the CPB), Khin Kyi (the widow of Thakin Ba Hein who had died in December 1946), and Hla Myaing (who surrendered in the 1950s and later became an editor of the state-run *Working People's Daily*). The congress resulted in the

---

[20]For detailed accounts of the Than Tun-Soe and CPB-AFPFL splits, see Josef Silverstein: *Burmese Politics—The Dilemma of National Unity* (New Brunswick, NJ: Rutgers University Press, 1980), p. 175. For Thakin Thein Pe's own account of his break with the CPB, see his "Critique of the Communist Movement in Burma," in *Documents on Communism*, ed. Fleischmann, pp. 241–43.

dismissal of the former moderate CPI secretary P. C. Joshi and the election of the much more militant B. T. Ranadive.

Some historians claim that this congress—and a meeting of the Southeast Asian Youth Conference, called under the auspicies of the World Federation of Democratic Youth and the International Union of Students which took place in Calcutta at the same time—were used by the newly formed Cominform to draw up a master plan for armed Communist insurrections all over Southeast Asia. This theory is based on the fact that Soviet spokesman Andrei Zhdanov had given a speech on the occasion of the founding of the Cominform at Wiliza Gora in Poland on September 22, 1947, advocating a much more confrontational line than the world Communist movement had followed since World War II. The world had become divided into two camps, Zhdanov declared: one was made up of the United States, Britain, France, and other "imperialist" powers, while the other belonged to the Soviet Union and the newly established "people's democracies." Other nations and movements must support this second camp if they were to have Communist support and sympathy.

This line was introduced to, and to a large extent also accepted by, the delegates at the Calcutta youth conference. But there is no evidence to support the claim that the meetings in Calcutta in February 1948 initiated armed Communist rebellions in Southeast Asia.[21] Thakin Ba Thein Tin also dismisses this notion and claims that the decison to take up arms on March 28 of that year was solely the CPB's own and was unrelated to the almost simultaneous uprisings in Malaya and the Philippines.[22] He says the only foreign representatives at the Calcutta congress were the six CPB delegates, two members of the central committee of the Communist League of Yugoslavia (who returned home after the congress; they did not, as claimed by some historians, go to Burma),[23] and Lance Sharkey, the general secretary of the Australian Communist Party. The only "outsider" Thakin Ba Thein Tin can remember meeting in Calcutta was a young Russian woman who was introduced to him as "Comrade Olga."[24] According to Thakin Ba Thein Tin, the question of armed struggle was not even discussed, and there were no representatives from Malaya, the Philippines, or Vietnam at the CPI congress—although some youths from Malaya, Vietnam, Indonesia, Ceylon, India, Pakistan, Nepal, and the Philippines attended the Calcutta youth conference. The Philippine delegates on their return home denounced the meeting as "Soviet-dominated."[25]

It is, however, plausible to assume that the radicalization of, for instance, the CPI and the CPB that followed arose from a confrontation during the youth meeting, which was also attended by representatives from Burma's AFPFL and the Indian Congress Party. The young Communists argued that the leaders of their

---

[21]Ruth T. McVey: *The Calcutta Conference and the Southeast Asian Uprisings* (Ithaca, NY: Cornell Modern Indonesia Project, Interim Report Series, 1958), p. 10. For another version of the Calcutta meetings, see McLane, *Soviet Strategies*, pp. 351–71.

[22]Interview with Thakin Ba Thein Tin, Panghsang, December 23, 1986.

[23]See for instance John F. Cady, *A History of Modern Burma* (Ithaca and London: Cornell University Press, 1958), p. 582. The information that Goshal attended the CPI congress in Calcutta is also incorrect.

[24]Olga Chechetkina, a Soviet journalist specializing in Indonesia, was present at the Calcutta meeting, according to McVey, *Calcutta Conference*, p. 2.

[25]Ibid., pp. 7 and 9.

respective countries had achieved a "sham independence" by collaborating with "the imperialists"—which prompted the delegates from the AFPFL and the Congress Party to walk out in protest. The fact that Joshi had been replaced by Ranadive also showed that, in general, the Communists in Asia were becoming more militant—but this seems to have been inspired more by internal developments in the countries of the region than by Zhdanov's speech in Poland at about the same time. In India, for instance, a rural rebellion had broken out in Telengana in Hyderabad State in 1946 and was still continuing when the Calcutta meetings were held. Ranadive even said in his report to the CPI's Second Congress: "Telengana today means Communists, and Communists mean Telengana."[26] The idea of a revolution based on the peasants had also taken firm root in China, from where it was spreading to Southeast Asia.

It is also possible that the CPB grossly overestimated its own strength and importance at this time—a feeling that may have been reinforced by the international contacts the Burmese Communists now were forging. Shortly after their return from Calcutta, Thakin Ba Thein Tin and others attended a mass peasant rally in Pyinmana; the enthusiasm there was unmistakable when party worker H. N. Goshal promised the peasants free land and no taxes. This was one of Goshal's rare appearances in the countryside; he had taken over the ABTUC after Thakin Ba Hein's death and concentrated on organizing the largely ethnic Indian working class in Rangoon. "Comrade Olga" also attended the Pyinmana meeting as an observer, as did one of the Malays who had participated in the youth conference in Calcutta. At a "resistance rally" held in Maha Bandoola Square in Rangoon on March 27 to commemorate the uprising against the Japanese, Thakin Than Tun spoke to a crowd of 3,000 workers.

H. N. Goshal had visited India shortly before the CPI's Second Congress and had become familiar with the changes which were taking place within the Communist movements in Asia. While in India, he purportedly prepared a thesis, outlining the future strategy of the Burmese Communists. The document, popularly known as the "Goshal Thesis," advocated "military training . . . in partisan warfare," and marked a clear break with the CPB's previous "Browderist" line. There is some uncertainty attached to the question of the document's authenticity since it was never published by the CPB and was distributed in Rangoon only by other sources, notably Thakin Thein Pe who broke with the party in March.[27] But whatever the case, the government in Rangoon was becoming increasingly concerned about the changes in the CPB's policy. Consequently, Kyaw Nyein, now independent Burma's home minister, ordered the arrest of the CPB's top leaders on the night of March 27.

The following morning, the car which usually picked up the CPB leaders at their homes to take them to the office did not appear. Thakin Ba Thein Tin sent one of his men to party headquarters at 130 Bargyar Street—to learn that it had been raided by the police. At 11.30 am, the Politbureau—Thakin Than Tun, Thakin Ba Thein Tin, and Goshal—held an emergency meeting. An order was issued, instructing all party workers in Rangoon, except underground agents, to leave for rural areas. According to CPB sources, there had been differences of opinion within the

---

[26]Sumanta Banerjee, *In the Wake of Naxalbari* (Calcutta: Subarnarekha, 1980), p. 82.

[27]For a full text of the so-called "Goshal Thesis," see Fleischmann, ed., *Documents on Communism*, pp. 83–128.

CPB's top leadership prior to this decision. Goshal had argued that Rangoon should be seized first by means of general strikes and mass rallies; Thakin Than Tun and Thakin Ba Thein Tin had favored the Maoist strategy of building up base areas in the countryside and then surrounding the cities, which should be captured later.[28] This seems to contradict the assumption that Goshal was the author of the famous thesis outlining a revolutionary strategy for Burma.

By April 1948 all the CPB leaders had left Rangoon and taken refuge in rural areas. The first shots were fired on April 2 in Paukkongyi in Pegu district; Burma's civil war, which was to continue up to the present, had begun. The decision to take up arms was confirmed by the party leadership at a Central Commitee meeting at Kyaukgyipauk in Toungoo district in May. The entire Central Committee, with the sole exception of Goshal, supported the Maoist strategy of rural guerrilla warfare as opposed to general strikes. Burma, in their analysis, was a "semi-colonial, semi-feudal" society which was not ripe for a proletarian revolution. Since then, for ideological reasons the CPB has paid little or no attention to struggles in urban areas; this quickly deprived the party of the comparatively widespread support it had previously enjoyed, especially among railway workers, dockworkers, miners, the laborers in the oil fields, and clerical workers. Nonetheless, the CPB remained a potent factor in Burmese politics, and underground cells were active in Rangoon and other urban centers throughout the 1950s.

The CPB generally divided the armed struggle that followed into five different periods. 1948–1955 were the years of intensive armed struggle during which the party controlled large large areas in the countryside of central Burma; 1955–1963 was a period of "rightist mistakes," i.e., the leadership showed willingness to compromise with the Rangoon government; 1963–1968 was the preparatory period for the thrust into the northeast which was then being mapped out in Beijing. During 1968–1975, a new base area was established east of the Salween river in northeastern Shan and Kachin States. In 1975, the CPB began implementing a plan codenamed "7510" (October 1975) with the aim of crossing the Salween and linking the northeastern base areas with the old strongholds in central Burma. The plan never materialized, and its failure ultimately led to the downfall of the CPB.

1948–1955: The Communist uprising spread quickly across the country; within a year the CPB could raise an estimated 15,000 armed partisans under the banner of the People's Liberation Army of Burma (PLAB).[29] Several well-known Burmese personalities joined the CPB in the underground, including two of the Thirty Comrades: Bo Ye Htut and Bo Yan Aung. Thakin Chit, a PRP leader, had gone over to the CPB in 1946. In addition, two of the five battalions which the Burmese Army had been permitted to form under the Kandy Agreement mutinied. The 1st and 3rd Burma Rifles, along with the No. 3 General Transport company in Mingaladon, set up the Revolutionary Burma Army (RBA) and allied themselves with the Communists. The mutineers numbered about 3,000 and were led by Bo Zeya, one of the Thirty

---

[28]Thakin Ba Thein Tin stated in an interview at Panghsang on December 24, 1986: "When I returned from [the CPI congress in] Calcutta, I found that Goshal was trying to seize Rangoon by propagating a general strike, holding mass meetings and advocating similar methods. I objected to this, arguing that we would have to seize the rural areas first, surround the urban centers and then capture the actual towns and cities."

[29]According to Thakin Ba Thein Tin, Panghsang, December 24, 1986. Cady puts the figure at 25,000 (*History of Modern Burma*, p. 583).

Comrades. In July 1948 the PVO split and one faction, renamed the People's Comrade Party (PCP), turned against the government. The Karen minority rose up in arms on January 31, 1949 to be followed by smaller bands of Pa-Os, Karennis, Mons, and Muslim *mujaheeds* in the Arakan region near East Pakistan (now Bangladesh).

Most of the Communists' attacks were initially carried out in Pegu district just north of Rangoon, but in March 1949 a combined CPB-Karen force managed to overrun Mandalay and hold it for a few weeks. Thayetmyo, Prome, Tharrawaddy, and a number of other towns were also briefly occupied by the rebels. This was in part made possible because one of the Burmese Army's ablest commanders, Naw Seng—a Kachin who had been decorated by the British for his role in fighting the Japanese during World War II—defected to the Karen rebels in February 1949. He became the overall commander of the "Upper Burma Campaign," involving Communist as well as ethnic insurgents who overran almost the entire country. Naw Seng, however, marched on Kachin State to start an uprising among his own ethnic group—but he and a few hundred of his followers were cornered by the Burmese Army near Möng Ko in northeastern Shan State in 1950. They retreated across the border into China, where they were disarmed, granted unofficial asylum by the Chinese, and allowed to settle in Guizhou province.

It is hardly surprising that the hastily conceived and badly coordinated "Upper Burma Campaign" failed. The Rangoon government received massive military aid from India which enabled it to reorganize its shattered forces and strike back against the highly disorganized rebels. The latter regrouped on September 1, 1950; the CPB's PLAB and the RBA merged to become the *pyithu tatmadaw* (ပြည်သူ့ တပ်မတော်), or the People's Army. Thakin Than Tun was appointed "supreme commander" and Bo Zeya chief of staff. At the same time, the policy of attacking towns—only to have to give them up again when the government launched counter-offensives—came under severe attack, since it did not conform with the Maoist thesis of "occupying the countryside first and surrounding the cities later." The last attacks on urban centers took place in late 1950 at Lewe and in early 1951 at Natawgyi near Myingyan. The Communists failed to occupy these towns, and after this concentrated their efforts on establishing guerrilla zones in rural areas.[30]

For strategic purposes, the new People's Army was divided into four divisions. The first had the Northern Pegu Yoma area, Pyinmana, Magwe, and Prome as its area of operation. The second covered the countryside around Kyaukse, Myingyan, Sagaing, and Mandalay in upper Burma. The third division operated in the Southern Pegu Yoma area and around Toungoo, Pegu, Hanthawaddy, and Rangoon. In addition, there were local brigades in the Irrawaddy Delta region, in Tenasserim in the southeast, and around Katha in the north. The Arakan region had no brigades, only local militia forces.[31]

Since 1949, the Communist insurgents had begun to confiscate land from big landowners to distribute it to landless peasants, something they first had done immediately after World War II. This "agrarian revolution" was confined to the

---

[30]Interview with Thakin Ba Thein Tin, Panghsang, December 24, 1986.

[31]Interview with Myo Myint, Panghsang, March 17, 1987. He gave the total strength of the People's Army in 1950 as 15,000, but added that the figure might have been 18,000 if local militia forces were included.

CPB-organized peasant rally in the late 1940s. Photo: CPB archives.

Thakin Than Tun, the first CPB chairman. Photo: CPB archives.

Pyinmana area, where as a result the CPB managed to win considerable popular support. But the defeat of the "Upper Burma Campaign" had severely demoralized the CPB's fighting force: victory, which had seemed close at hand, eluded them.

To address the crisis, in 1951 the CPB convened a Central Committee meeting in a village in Pyinmana district. The Chinese revolution had succeeded because the Communists had joined hands with the Kuomintang against the Japanese—and then turned against the foreign invader and driven the Kuomintang into exile in Taiwan and parts of northeastern Burma. At this time, there was a strong belief among some CPB cadres that a similiar strategy could be put into practice in Burma by forming a united front with the Rangoon government against Burma's "foreign invaders," i.e., the Kuomintang forces that had retreated across the frontier from Yunnan in 1949–1950. If successful, the Communists would gain a stronger position and then be able to turn against the government. A new line, branded "PCG" (Peace and Coalition Government), was suggested. As a reconciliatory gesture, the CPB began to return the land they had once distributed to the cultivators back to the landlords who had been affected by the Communists' "agrarian revolution." The inevitable outcome was that many CPB soldiers, who were sons of peasants, became disillusioned, left the *pyithu tatmadaw*, and returned to their home villages. The Rangoon government never accepted the CPB's offer of a united front—and the Communists lost nearly half of their fighting force in the process. The armed uprising against the government had failed.

1955–1963: The CPB's Central Committee held a second emergency meeting in 1955 at *Wayawngdaw Sakan*, or "the Bamboo Forest Camp," in the Saytouttaya area near the Arakan Yoma, west of Minbu. It was attended by nearly all of the leaders of Burma's Communist underground: Thakin Than Tun, Goshal, Bo Ye Htut, Thakin Tin Mya (who had left Thakin Soe's group and rejoined the main CPB), Thakin Chit, Thakin Zin, Dr. Nag (*yebaw* Tun Maung), Thakin Pe Tint, and several others. They re-evaluated the CPB's experiences of seven years of armed struggle and decided to adopt a completely new policy. Three conclusions were reached:

1) The CPB had become divorced from the people of Burma;
2) Therefore, the armed struggle should be abandoned, and the CPB should become a legal opposition party similar to the CPI in neighboring India;
3) After mobilizing and organizing the people and regaining its previous strength, the CPB could reconsider the possibility of armed struggle at a later stage.

Then came the 20th Congress of the Soviet Communist Party in 1956, and the news from Moscow reached the CPB's jungle hide-outs in Burma: Stalin had been denounced and the Soviets envisaged a "peaceful transition" to socialism. The entire PCP surrendered in 1957 along with many CPB cadres, including Thakin Tin Mya. Thakin Ba Thein Tin remembers: "This is what we call the 'revisionist line,' the liquidation of the armed struggle. We suffered severe set-backs, although our headquarters was still in the Pyinmana area. There was some fighting, but we were always on the run."[32]

---

[32]Interview with Thakin Ba Thein Tin, Panghsang, December 24, 1986.

Although the government did not legalize the CPB, its policy towards the Communists since the inception of armed struggle in 1948 had been a combination of military pressure and attempts to solve the problem by political means. To neutralize the threat posed by the CPB, then prime minister U Nu already in May 1948 had presented a "Leftist Unity Program," emphasizing land reform in rural areas and the introduction of a democratic local administration. To some extent, these tactics—combined with the CPB's own mistakes—had managed to undermine Communist influence in the rural areas. In May 1950, after having scored some successes on the battlefield, U Nu's government had issued an amnesty order, promising immunity to all insurgents who surrendered. The CPB was not formally outlawed until 1953.

After the CPB took to the jungle in 1948, its "mass organizations" were taken over mainly by organizers from the legal BSP, which almost formed "a party within the party" in the broader front, the AFPFL. The BSP retained many of the Communist symbols, but despite its affirmation of Marxism, a much closer parallel existed between it and and the British Labour Party. The Trade Union Congress (Burma) [TUC(B)] and the All-Burma Peasants' Organization (ABPO) both were closely affiliated to the BSP. But according to historian Hugh Tinker: "One great difference between British and Burmese socialism, however, lies in the influence within the British party of the trade unions and their hard-headed working-class leaders. The TUC(B) is little more than an appendix of the BSP and the leaders are, almost without exception, bourgeois intellectuals. Not one Socialist leader comes from a family of 'workers' or 'peasants'.... Some of the socialists came to politics through journalism, the law, teaching, or business; none worked their way up from the ranks of manual labour."[33]

There was, however, a sharp division between the moderate BSP leaders Kyaw Nyein and Ba Swe, and trade unionist Thakin Lwin, who favored a more dogmatic Marxist line as well as closer ties with the Soviet bloc. The split became inevitable on May 1, 1950 when Thakin Lwin announced that the TUC(B) intended to join the now Soviet-sponsored World Federation of Trade Unions. On September 21, Thakin Lwin was expelled from the AFPFL. He responded on October 7 by withdrawing the TUC(B) from the AFPFL. Shortly afterwards, the BSP split; 43 party leaders denounced the main Ba Swe-Kyaw Nyein faction and set up the Burma Workers' and Peasants' Party (BWPP). Thakin Chit Maung, an ABPO leader, also joined the new party. In 1955, the BWPP and other leftist organizations—as well as some moderate anti-AFPFL groups—combined to set up the National Unity Front (NUF) which contested in the 1956 elections. It did extremely well capturing 30.4 percent of the vote and 48 seats in the 250-member lower house of the Burmese parliament. The leftist factor in Burmese politics was further reinforced in 1957 when, with the surrender of the PCP, many of its former cadres joined the NUF.[34]

The BWPP was sometimes described as a "legal Communist party," and it has been assumed that the relationship between the BWPP and the CPB was in some ways similar to the present situation in the Philippines, where the underground Communist Party of the Philippines has a legal arm, the Bayan or People's Party. Thakin Chit Maung, however, denies that the BWPP ever had any direct links with the CPB, while admitting that the policies of the two parties had many sim-

---

[33]Hugh Tinker: *The Union of Burma* (London: Oxford University Press, 1957), pp. 63–64.
[34]Ibid., p. 90.

ilarities.[35] A better analogy would be the legal Communist parties in India. Hardly surprisingly, Thakin Ba Thein Tin considered the BWPP "rightist deviationists" because they had accepted the parliamentary system.[36] Nonetheless, there were frequent allegations that the BWPP received some clandestine support from the Soviet Embassy in Rangoon.[37]

The CPB at this time was at any rate too weak to play a significant role in national Burmese politics. In 1958, the government launched a major operation, code-named *Aung Marga* ("Victory Path") against the CPB remnants in northern Burma. The Shwebo area was cleared of insurgents, and the CPB cadres and troops who were still holding out retreated to the Pegu Yoma mountain range, just north of the capital. This had previously been a retreat base for guerrilla units operating in the Pyinmana area, but from 1959 onwards it became the site of the CPB's general headquarters. It was a poor mountain area with only fourteen villages—mostly Karen—and rice had to be collected from the plains below. A veteran from the Pegu Yoma remembers that the approximately 1,000 guerrillas there "were constantly hungry. It was quite all right when we lay down, but we got dizzy when we had to stand up. But even so, our morale was high and we all believed in a red future for Burma."[38]

While the legal leftist organizations were gaining some support in Rangoon and other cities and the CPB's once powerful insurgent army was crumbling in the jungles, some Burmese Communists had chosen a completely different path. When the CPB forces had been driven back from the urban areas towards the end of 1951, groups of Burmese Communists had begun trekking towards China to ask for military assistance. Already in 1950, the CPB had set up a base area in Katha District in upper Burma, south of Bhamo in Kachin State, ready to link up with the Chinese. If aid was funneled across the border, the CPB planned to operate from the Shweli River in northern Shan State, and from there push down towards Mandalay and Burma proper.

The first batch of about thirty CPB cadres, led by *yebaw* Aung Gyi, left for Yunnan in 1951. In May 1953, Thakin Ba Thein Tin, then vice party chairman, reached Tengchong after an arduous year-long journey by elephant and on foot. One more group followed, bringing the total of CPB cadres in China to 143. Among them were also Bo Zeya, the chief of staff of the CPB army, Politbureau member Thakin Than Myaing, and Thakin Bo, a senior member of the Central Committee. They were well received by the Chinese and allowed to remain in Sichuan province where they were given political training. But no military aid was forthcoming at this stage; China was not willing to sacrifice its friendly relations with the U Nu government for the sake of the CPB. The Communist failure in Burma can partly be attributed to the strength displayed by the U Nu government's persistent, actively neutral foreign policy.[39]

---

[35]Interview with Thakin Chit Maung, Rangoon, April 20, 1989.

[36]Interview with Thakin Ba Thein Tin, Panghsang, December 24, 1986.

[37]Tinker, *Union of Burma*, p. 91.

[38]Interview with Aung Sein and Than Maung, two Pegu Yoma survivors, Panghsang, December 25, 1986.

[39]John H. Badgley, "Burma's Radical Left: A Study in Failure," *Problems of Communism* 10, 2 (March–April 1961): 47.

Much to their surprise, the newly arrived CPB members were introduced to an old comrade who had disappeared almost a decade earlier: Aye Ngwe, a Sino-Burman ex-student from Rangoon. When it became clear that Aung San had failed to reach Communist-controlled areas of China in 1941, the CPB in Rangoon had sent Aye Ngwe overland to Yunnan. He had walked across the border bridge at Kyuhkok-Wanting in September 1941. It had taken five years for Aye Ngwe to make contact with the Communist Party of China (CPC)—by which time he had lost touch with the CPB. In 1947, he had become a member of the CPC and learned Chinese. When the CPB cadres began arriving from Burma in the early 1950s, Aye Ngwe was called in to act as interpreter.

The Burmese Communists also attended courses in Marxism-Leninism at Beijing's higher party school. Three promising younger cadres ware selected to further their studies in Moscow in 1957. These were Khin Maung Gyi, an intellectual from Rangoon who had been active in the Left-leaning All-Burma Students' Union; San Thu, a party worker from Pyawbwe in central Burma; and Aung Win, a junior party member. In Moscow, they were joined by two other young Burmese Communists, Kyaw Zaw and Thein Aung (*yebaw* Lwin). Khin Maung Gyi was the most outstanding of the five. He attended the Academy of Social Sciences in Moscow and wrote a thesis on "Agrarian Problems in Burma."

The Burmese authorities were most probably unaware of the presence of a fairly large number of CPB members in China and the Soviet Union—at least, they did not know who they were and what they were doing. Nevertheless, the "Communist spectre" had become an important ingredient in Burmese politics. When U Nu handed over power to the army chief, General Ne Win, on October 28, 1958, the supposed threat of the insurgents was one of the reasons given for allowing the military to set up a caretaker government. During the fight against the insurgents—and the Kuomintang invaders—in the early 1950s, the initially tiny Burmese Army had had to be rebuilt and had gradually emerged as a potent factor in Burmese politics. In 1955, it had even formulated its own policy which strongly resembled the *dwifungsi* ("dual function") doctrine of the Indonesian Army, which asserted that the military has both a defense and social-political role. A document titled "The National Ideology and the Role of the Defence Services" spoke of psychological regeneration which was the result of the "decisive leadership of the government and the clarity and conviction of the Defence Services."[40]

In a speech before Parliament on October 31, 1958, Ne Win alleged that "the rebels were increasing their activities, and the political pillar was collapsing. It was imperative that the Union should not drown in shallow waters as it nearly did in 1948–1949. So it fell on the armed forces to perform their bounden duty to take all security measures to forestall and prevent a recurrence."[41] To anybody familiar with the near-collapse of the CPB during the period 1955–1957, this seemed mere humbug and a flimsy excuse for the formation of the military caretaker government. But this line was also played up by Sein Win, then editor of the *Guardian*, a well-respected daily newspaper in Rangoon which was secretly funded by the army. Sein

---

[40]*The National Ideology and Role of the Defence Services*, adopted at the Defence Services Conference, Meiktila, October 21, 1958. For a commentary on this document, see Jan Becka, *The Origin and Role of the National Armed Forces in Burma's Struggle for Independence*, vol. 49 (Prague: Archív Orientální, Academica Praha, 1981), pp. 362–63.

[41]Maung Maung, *Burma and General Ne Win* (Bombay: Asia Publishing House, 1969), p. 248.

Win wrote a pamphlet called *The Split Story* which tried to justify the army's role in Burmese politics, playing up the alleged Communist threat: "Despite the official banning of the Communist party, Communists still exist above ground in various guises." A split within the AFPFL in 1958—which preceded the formation of a military caretaker government—would otherwise have "paved the way for the Communist ascension to power," according to Sein Win.[42]

In reality, it was the military's decision to intervene in the political process in Burma which paved the way for the re-emergence of the CPB—or, more precisely, prompted China to decide on open support for the Burmese Communists. The caretaker government resigned after general elections had been held in February–March 1960. These elections gave a landslide victory to U Nu who once again formed a civilian cabinet. His *Pyidaungsu* (Union) party (born out of his "Clean AFPFL" faction following the 1958 split) captured 52.7 percent of the vote. The other, "Stable" faction, which was favored by the military received 29.8 percent, and the previously powerful NUF captured a mere 5.4 percent It seemed as if Burma's parliamentary system had won, and that the military, as well as the legal leftist parties, had been defeated.

But, once again, using the question of "national unity" and "threats posed by insurgents," the army stepped in a second time on March 2, 1962. This time they were there to stay and had no intention of holding general elections or returning power to a civilian government. The students were the first to protest against the military takeover. Although they demonstrated peacefully, troops were sent to Rangoon University to quell the protests. On July 6–7, 1962 government troops opened fire on the demonstrators. Officially, fifteen students were killed; unofficial estimates put the death toll in the hundreds. The CPB's ragged forces in the Pegu Yoma were unexpectedly boosted by the arrival of scores of young intellectuals who wanted to take up arms against the new military régime.

1963–1968: A new era in Burmese insurgency was ushered in after the 1962 coup d'etat. The ethnic rebellions, primarily in Shan and Kachin states, flared anew—and for the first time the CPB began receiving open support from China. The military takeover had upset the regional stability provided by Burma's neutral democratic government; furthermore, China had long been wary of the ambitious and sometimes unpredictable Ne Win. Six important events took place immediately after the coup in Rangoon:

1) The CPB was for the first time allowed to print propaganda leaflets and other material in Beijing. Already on August 1, 1962, the Beijing- and Sichuan-based exiles published a document titled *Some Facts about Ne Win's Military Government*, denouncing the new régime.

2) The most urgent task was to find a way to contact the CPB units in the Pegu Yoma and other places in central Burma, as there had been no links between them and the group in China since the latter had trekked to Yunnan in the early 1950s. By a strange twist of historical events, it was the new military regime in Rangoon that unwittingly provided an opportunity for the CPB exiles in China to re-establish these links. Probably hoping that the insurgents would give up when faced with the massive force of the military government, it called for peace talks after about a year in power. From July 14, 1963, the CPB, Thakin Soe's much smaller Red

---

[42]Sein Win, *The Split Story* (Rangoon: The Guardian Ltd., 1959), p. 67.

Flag Communist party, the Karen, Mon, Shan, Kachin rebel armies, and some smaller groups attended the negotiations in Rangoon, with guarantees of free and safe passage to and from the peace parley, regardless of the outcome.

The colorful Thakin Soe probably attracted the most attention when he arrived accompanied by a team of attractive young girls in khaki uniforms He placed a portrait of Stalin in front of him on the negotiating table and then began attacking the revisionism of Soviet leader Khrushchev and the opportunism of Mao Zedong's China. Thakin Soe was soon excluded from the talks. However, twenty-nine veterans from the main CPB in China also arrived in Rangoon, purportedly to participate in the peace talks. Among the "Beijing Returnees," as they came to be known, were *yebaw* Aung Gyi, Thakin Bo, Bo Zeya—and Thakin Ba Thein Tin who did not actually participate in the talks but seized the opportunity to visit the CPB's headquarters in the Pegu Yoma, bringing with him radio transmitters and other aid from China.[43]

According to CPB documents, the government demanded that the Communists should concentrate all their troops and party members inside an area stipulated by the authorities, inform the government if there were any remaining guerrillas or cadres elsewhere, stop all organizational activities of the party, and cease fund raising.[44] The intransigence of the military régime was a blessing in disguise for the CPB. The talks broke down on November 14, and the various insurgents returned to their respective jungle camps. Thakin Ba Thein Tin and another CPB cadre returned to Beijing, while the other twenty-seven returnees stayed in the Pegu Yoma where they assumed *de facto* leadership of the party at home.

3) Following the split within the international Communist movement at about the same time, Khin Maung Gyi, San Thu, and Thein Aung returned to Beijing in November 1963. Aung Win and Kyaw Zaw, who had married Russian women, stayed on in Moscow. A "leading group of five" to direct the work in China was set up in Beijing shortly after Thakin Ba Thein Tin's return from the peace talks in Rangoon. This group, which became the nucleus of the new leadership of the CPB which emerged during the 1960s, consisted of Thakin Ba Thein Tin as "leader," Khin Maung Gyi as his personal secretary, and Thakin Than Myaing, Than Shwe, and Tin Yee as members. Than Shwe was a World War II veteran who had been educated at an officers' training school in Rangoon during the initial stages of the Japanese occupation; Tin Yee was a CPB cadre from Pegu who had joined the party in 1943 during the anti-Japanese struggle. Both had gone to China in the early 1950s.

4) In late 1963, San Thu, one of the Moscow returnees, was put in charge of a team that began surveying possible infiltration routes from Yunnan into northeastern Burma. During this period, China built a new network of asphalted highways, leading from Kunming to various points along the borders with Burma and with Laos, where another Communist movement was active.

5) Nearly all the CPB cadres in China—with the exception of Than Shwe and a few others—were well-read Marxist intellectuals with little or no experience in military matters. But Naw Seng and his 200–300 Kachins had been living as ordinary citizens in Guizhou since they had retreated to China in 1950; in early 1963—

---

[43]Interview with Thakin Ba Thein Tin, Panghsang, December 24, 1986; with Aung Sein and Than Maung, Panghsang, December 25, 1986.

[44]*A Short Outline*, p. 4.

even before the peace talks in Rangoon—Naw Seng was brought to Sichuan. He was introduced to Thakin Ba Thein Tin and told that the time had come to go back to Burma and fight. Naw Seng, eager to leave his people's commune in Guizhou, readily agreed. He assembled his men and their military skills were rehearsed at a training camp in Yunnan. Aye Ngwe gave them political lectures in Marxism-Leninism.

6) The small cells of ethnic Chinese Communists were for the first time put in touch with the CPB. They were few in number, but the Chinese embassy in Rangoon arranged for ethnic Chinese from the capital and for some small towns in the Irrawaddy Delta to go to the CPB's then base area along the Shweli river (and later to the new northeastern base area which was set up after 1968). The number increased after anti-Chinese communal riots in Rangoon in 1967.[45] These riots also provided the catalyst for the already planned China-sponsored CPB thrust into Shan State.

The Beijing-based CPB declared in 1964: "the CPB is struggling against revisionism or right-wing opportunism as the main danger in the international Communist movement and inside our party."[46] Internationally, the CPB stance was reflected in its fierce verbal attacks on the "Khrushchev revisionists"; at home by bloody purges in the Pegu Yoma. The Beijing returnees, inspired by China's Cultural Revolution and assigned the task of "cleansing" the party in preparation for the momentous events that were being planned in Beijing, staged grisly mass trials in the Pegu Yoma. They enlisted the support of miltant young *tat ni lunge* (တပ်နီ လူငယ်), or "Red Guards," who often were orphans raised by the party and led to regard it as their "parent," and hence were immensely loyal to their new masters. *Yebaw Htay*, who had headed the CPB's delegation to the 1963 peace talks, was branded "Burma's Deng Xiaoping" and executed. The veteran Goshal was denounced as "Burma's Liu Shaoqi" and also killed—as was Bo Yan Aung, one of the Thirty Comrades. The third of the wartime heroes who had joined the CPB, Bo Ye Htut, had already surrendered in 1963 and escaped punishment.

Many of the intellectuals who had joined the CPB in the wake of the 1962 coup d'etat were purged and killed as well. This policy was unofficially referred to as *pyouk-touk-hta* (ဖြုတ် ထုတ် သတ်), or "the Three Ds," namely "Dismissed from office; Dispelled from the party; and Disposed of (i.e. executed)." Thakin Ba Thein Tin refers to the purges as "the Revolution within the party" and claims that no more than fifty-three people were executed.[47] Among the exiles in China, Thakin

---

[45] In 1967 there were acute shortages of rice and basic foodstuffs in Rangoon. At the same time, the Chinese community in the capital had been influenced by the Cultural Revolution in China and many young Sino-Burmese began wearing red Mao badges. This violated an official Burmese regulation, and the young "Red Guards" were ordered to take off their badges. When some of them refused, anti-Chinese riots broke out in June and July that year. Chinese shops and homes were ransacked and looted, and many Sino-Burmese were killed.

[46] *A Short Outline*, p. 5.

[47] Interview with Thakin Ba Thein Tin, Panghsang, December 24, 1986. For a detailed and comparatively accurate account of the purges in the Pegu Yoma, see သခင်သန်း: ထွန်း: ၏ နောက်ဆုံး:နေ့ များ ("*The Last Days of Thakin Than Tun*," 2 vols. [Rangoon, 1969]) which ostensibly was written by some CPB defectors but the actual author is a former chief of Burma's military intelligence, Brig.-Gen. Tin Oo.

Than Myaing was also purged and languished in a Chinese labor camp until he was released and "rehabilitated" in 1973.[48]

One of the most hardline of the Beijing Returnees was Taik Aung, who had been born in a peasant family in Waw near Pegu and was considered a ruthless fanatic. Of the other Beijing returnees, Bo Zeya was killed in action in 1967 near Tharrawaddy, *yebaw* Aung Gyi fell in battle in 1968, and Thakin Bo died of illness in 1969. The CPB experienced five extremely bloody years before the master plan was put into practice.

---

[48]Several authors have assumed that Thakin Than Myaing was executed during the Cultural Revolution (for instance, Klaus Fleischmann: *Die Kommunistische Partei Birmas— Von den Anfängen bis zur Gegenwart* [Hamburg: Mitteilungen des Instituts für Asienkunde, 1989], p. 421). However, sources close to Thakin Than Myaing claim that he is still alive and lives in Sichuan, China.

THE NORTHEASTERN BASE AREA
1968–1988

Early in the morning of New Year's Day 1968, Naw Seng and his Kachins crossed the border into Burma. The incursion took place at Möng Ko, a small town on the Sino-Burmese frontier in northeastern Shan State—the very same place from which Naw Seng had retreated into China eighteen years earlier. But this time his 300 Kachins were heavily armed and well equipped, and they were guided by Than Shwe, Khin Maung Gyi, and other leading CPB cadres. Within hours the local Burmese Army garrison in Möng Ko was over-run. Heavy fighting continued in surrounding areas, and for the first time in the country's civil war the Burmese Army found itself outgunned and, in some cases, even outnumbered as thousands of Chinese "volunteers" streamed across the border to fight alongside the CPB.

In accordance with the plan, the CPB divided its new strongholds into a number of "War Zones":

303: This was the Möng Ko region west of the Salween river, the CPB's first base area in the northeast;

404: The Chinese-dominated Kokang district, east of Möng Ko and the Salween river, became the CPB's next target less than a week after Naw Seng's return. With local warlord Pheung Kya-shin as military commander and Tin Yee as political commissar, the CPB entered Kokang on January 5, 1968. Almost the entire area had been taken over within a year to become "War Zone 404";

202: This was the new name for the old guerrilla zone along the southern bank of the Shweli river—the route down to Mandalay and Burma proper. In 1968 a Burman from Monywa, Kyi Pyang, was sent to organize and rebuild the scattered units there into "War Zone 202";

101: When Naw Seng entered Möng Ko, he had expected to find only Burmese government troops in the area. But during his exile in China, his own Kachin people had organized the Kachin Independence Army (KIA); the Kachin-inhabited hills of northeastern Shan State, including Möng Ko, were one of its strongholds. Fierce fighting broke out between the CPB and the KIA, and halted the Communists' advance westwards. Fierce fighting raged between the CPB and the KIA until 1976 when a ceasefire eventually was reached between the two rebel armies. In Kachin State itself, however, Ting Ying and Zalum, two local commanders in the Kambaiti area, had defected to the CPB in May 1969, along with 400 men. This area became "War Zone 101." Naw Seng himself died in 1972 under circumstances which never have been satisfactorily explained. The official CPB version says that he died in a fall from a cliff in the Wa Hills while hunting in the forest. Many Kachins, however, believe that he was killed by the CPB because he did not want to fight against his own kin in the KIA.

Using these four War Zones as base areas, the CPB marched on to conquer place after place. Their usual tactics were to contact a local, tribal warlord who enjoyed considerable local support and respect but had little or no comprehension of ideological matters. In this way, after six years of heavy fighting, the CPB managed to wrest control over a 20,000 square kilometer area adjacent to the Chinese frontier, stretching uninterruptedly from the Mekong river and the Lao border up to the border town of Panghsai (Kyu-hkok) where the Burma Road crosses into Yunnan. North of this solid base area, the CPB controlled enclaves opposite Namkham in Shan State, as well as the Kambaiti area in Kachin State (for a detailed description of these areas and warlords, see Appendix II).

The Chinese poured more aid into the CPB effort than any other Communist movement outside Indochina. Unlike the old units in the Pegu Yoma, these new troops had new Chinese uniforms with red stars in their caps, and were well equipped with modern Chinese weapons: M-21 semiautomatic rifles, M-22 assault rifles, M-23 light machine-guns; 12.7mm anti-aircraft guns; 60, 82, and 120mm mortars; and 75mm recoilless rifles. Radio equipment, jeeps, trucks, petrol, and even rice, other foodstuffs, cooking oil, and kitchen utensils were sent across the frontier into the new northeastern base area. The Chinese also built hydroelectric power stations at Möng Ko as well as Panghsang, the headquarters of the northeastern forces. A clandestine radio station, the *People's Voice of Burma*, was officially inaugurated on March 28, 1971, the 23rd anniversary of the CPB's uprising, and began transmitting from the Yunnanese side of the frontier in April.

The CPB's only major defeat during this period was suffered at Kunlong, where a strategic bridge crosses the Salween (the only other bridge across this turbulent river is at Ta-Kaw on the Taunggyi-Kengtung road). A 42-day battle was fought from November 1971 to January 1972 at the river crossing. But the CPB failed to capture the bridge and suffered heavy casualties due to its Chinese-inspired human-wave attack tactics against the well entrenched government troops near Kunlong.

Despite its victory at Kunlong, the Burmese Army recognized that it would not be possible—at that point at least—to push the CPB back in northeastern Shan State. Instead, Rangoon turned its attention to the much weaker CPB areas in the Pegu Yoma and the Irrawaddy Delta to prevent Chinese aid from reaching these much more crucial areas in central Burma.

Important changes were also taking place in these old base areas. A radio-link between the Pegu Yoma and China had been established after Thakin Ba Thein Tin's visit in 1963, and in 1965 a prominent Central Committee member, Thakin Pe Tint, was sent overland to Yunnan to cement the ties between the units "at home" and the new "leading group of five" in Beijing. Aung Sein, a young Burmese Communist who had been a soldier in the group that had escorted Thakin Ba Thein Tin to China in 1953, was sent back along the same overland route to the Pegu Yoma in 1967, carrying a letter which revealed the "invasion plans" in detail, thus contrasted with 1963, when the Pegu Yoma-based headquarters had only been informed in general terms about what was going to happen.[1]

---

[1] Interview with the messenger, Aung Sein, Panghsang, December 25, 1986.

Portraits in Panghsang of Thakin Than Tun and Thakin Zin.
Photo: Hseng Noung Lintner.

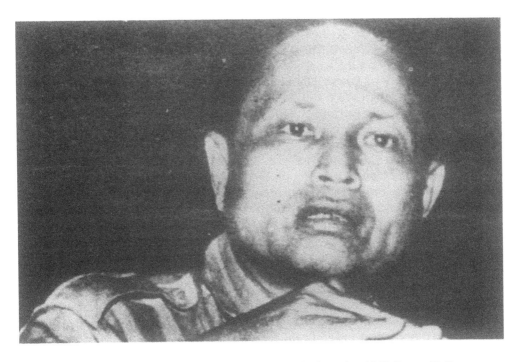

Thakin Soe (the Red Flag Communist leader) at the 1963 Peace Talks.
Photo: CPB Archives

The *pyouk-touk-hta* purges, however, had depleted the ranks of the units in the Pegu Yoma, and effectively alienated the CPB from the urban intelligentsia. On September 24, 1968—less than a year after the thrust into Möng Ko—the CPB's official chairman, Thakin Than Tun, was assassinated in the Pegu Yoma by a government infiltrator. He was succeeded by Thakin Zin, who tried to get help from the powerful northeastern forces to save the old stronghold. In 1969 "the Butcher" Taik Aung and about ten cadres were sent from the Pegu Yoma to Möng Ko. They did not return, since by 1970 the government offensive against the CPB's central strongholds was in full swing. Communist as well as Karen insurgents were forced to evacuate the Irrawaddy Delta in 1970–1971 and the Pinlebu area in the north was cleared of CPB influence by 1971–1972. The old Red Flag faction—never very influential in any case—almost vanished after its maverick leader, Thakin Soe, was captured in November 1970 at his last stronghold, a tiny camp on the northern fringes of the Arakan Yoma mountain range. He was taken to Rangoon and jailed.

In early 1975 a major operation was launched in the Pegu Yoma, still officially the CPB's headquarters. The Burmese Army's crack 77th Light Infantry Division—the first in a series of special units set up to combat the Communists and other insurgents—overran the CPB's old bases in the Yoma and even managed to kill Thakin Zin and his secretary, Thakin Chit, on March 15. The morale of the Burmese Army was boosted: the scheme to link up the northeastern base areas with the old strongholds in central Burma had failed. Chinese arms reached only the Kyawkku-Nawng Long-Nawng Wu area in western Shan State, or "War Zone 108" as it became known.

At about the same time anti-government protests swept central Burma. On May 13, 1974, the oil workers at Chauk had gone on strike demanding higher wages. The unrest spread from the oil fields—the origin of the historic anti-British movement of the 1930s—to Rangoon. Railway workers and laborers at a spinning mill in the capital went on strike on June 6. The government responded by sending in troops, who fired indiscriminately on the workers. More unrest erupted towards the end of the year, when the body of former UN Secretary General U Thant was flown back to Burma for burial. Rangoon's traditionally militant students seized the opportunity to launch massive anti-government demonstrations. The army were called in again, and scores of students were killed when the troops sprayed automatic rifle fire into the crowds. The unrest continued for more than a year until the government had forced the opposition into submission.

The government blamed the protests on "unscrupulous elements from the outside who had created disturbances," and made vague references to the Communists. Unlike in 1962, this time there was no exodus of intellectuals to the CPB's base area, despite the fact that the Communists were now much stronger than ever before. This was not only because the Communists, following the *pyouk-touk-hta* purges, had managed to alienate themselves from the urban population: to encourage urban unrest also ran contrary to the CPB's Maoist strategy, the essence of which still was to establish strongholds in the rural areas in order to surround the towns and the cities. Significantly, the CPB only assigned one not very senior cadre, Zaw Win, to liaise with the students in Rangoon. Although he managed to woo a few over to the CPB side, the number was insignificant compared to the thousands of Burmese intellectuals who flocked to the Thai border, where followers of deposed Prime Minister U Nu were organizing resistance against the military régime.

Instead, the CPB was busy reorganizing itself and re-mapping its military tactics following the loss of the central base areas. After the death of Thakin Zin and Thakin Chit, a new, extended Central Committee was elected. From 1975 onwards, the "northeastern group" became the official, and not only the *de facto*, leadership of the CPB. Thakin Ba Thein Tin was elected the new chairman and Khin Maung Gyi became party secretary. The new Central Committee also included Taik Aung and Myo Myint, another Pegu Yoma veteran who had made it to the northeast. Then, in October 1975, a new plan, code-named "7510" (October 1975) was drawn up. The aim was to extend the northeastern base area, east of the Salween, to the areas west of the river, and then to try to re-enter central Burma and rebuild the lost strongholds there.

But in order to do this, alliances with the non-Communist, ethnic rebel groups west of the Salween were imperative. Ties were forged with the Shan State Army (SSA) and smaller bands of Pa-O, Padaung (Kayan) and Kayah (Karenni) rebels. These groups benefitted from arms supplies from the CPB in return for allowing the Communists to operate in their respective areas. A new brigade, 683, was set up for this purpose. It was commanded by Li Ziru, one of the Chinese volunteers who had joined the CPB in 1968. He crossed the Salween towards the end of 1975, and in February 1977 the 683 Brigade reached the Loi Tsang mountain range in western Shan State, overlooking the old Kyawkku-Nawng Long-Nawng Wu stronghold. The scheme failed, however, mainly because of lack of popular support for the CPB. The Shans and other minority peoples in the area still favored the non-Communist rebel groups. As a result, the latter were forced to sever their ties with the CPB in order not to lose the support they were still enjoying. This led to splits within several of the smaller rebel armies. But the most important political outcome was the fact that the CPB was unable to implement "Plan 7510."

The CPB's policy towards the power struggle which at this time was raging in China also had an immediate impact on limiting the CPB's expansion. In April 1976, when China's radical Left reasserted itself and ousted Deng Xiaoping, the CPB—unlike other Communist parties in the region—spoke out loudly in favor of the hardliners: "The revisionist clique [with which Deng was linked] headed by Liu Shaoqi has been defeated," the CPB stated in a congratulatory message to the 55th anniversary of the CPC in June 1976. It went on: "The movement to repulse the Right deviationist attempt at reversing correct verdicts, and the decision of the Central Committee of the CPC on measures taken against rightist chieftain Deng Xiaoping are in full accord with Marxism-Leninism, Mao Zedong thought."[2]

In a second message, mourning the death of Mao Zedong in September 1976, the CPB stated: "Guided by Chairman Mao Zedong's proletarian revolutionary line, the Chinese people seized great victories in the socialist revolution and socialist construction in the Great Proletarian Cultural Revolution, in criticizing Liu Shaoqi's counter-revolutionary revisionist line, in criticizing Lin Biao and Confucius and in criticizing Deng Xiaoping and repulsing the Right deviationist attempt at reversing correct verdicts and consolidating the dictatorship of the proletariat, thus, consolidating the People's republic of China—the reliable bulwark of the world proletarian revolution."[3]

---

[2]*Beijing Review*, July 30, 1976.
[3]Ibid., September 30, 1976.

The CPB had reason to re-evaluate the reliability of that bulwark the following year when Deng re-assumed power in Beijing. The CPB, which once had branded its own "revisionists" *yebaw* Htay and Goshal as "Burma's Deng Xiaoping" and "Burma's Liu Shaoqi" respectively, fell silent. The *Beijing Review* and other official Chinese publications, which had previously published battle news and CPB documents, stopped printing anything about the "revolutionary struggle in Burma." The CPB was mentioned for the last time in November 1976 when Thakin Ba Thein Tin and Thakin Pe Tint had called on Hua Guofeng in Beijing.[4]

The Burmese military quickly and shrewdly exploited the rift by lending its good offices to China in Cambodia, which by then had become the focus of Chinese interest as concern in Beijing increased over Vietnam's designs on its Indochinese neighbor. In December 1977, Ne Win became the first foreign head of state to visit Phnom Penh after the Khmer Rouge takeover. The Chinese were no doubt behind the unusual visit, hoping to draw the Khmer Rouge out of its diplomatic isolation. Ne Win played along, hoping for his part that Beijing would further reduce its support for the CPB. He was not disappointed. In 1978, the CPB's entire China-based central office, including the broadcasting station, the *People's Voice of Burma*, was forced to return to Panghsang, its official general headquarters since the fall of Pegu Yoma in 1975. The Chinese "volunteers" were also recalled.

Faced with this new situation, the CPB Central Committee met, first at Möng Ko and later at Panghsang, between November 1978 and June 1979. The party's 40th anniversary on August 15, 1979 was subdued. In a lengthy speech, Thakin Ba Thein Tin emphasized that the party must be "self-reliant" and, without being specific, said that the CPB "had made many mistakes" during its 40-year long history. In other announcements, "non-interference" was declared to be a major aspect of the CPB's relations with "fraternal Communist parties."[5]

On November 19 the Burmese Army launched its first big counter-offensive in the northeast, code-named *Min Yan Aung-I* (King Conqueror-I). The aim was to capture Panghsang "before Christmas." Although the operation fell short of that objective, the Burmese Army managed to regain control over a large area known as Mawhpa. A forward base was established at Loi Hsia-Kao mountain, less than 30 kilometers west of Panghsang. The CPB claims that the government forces suffered 2,085 dead, 3,537 wounded, and 320 prisoners of war before the offensive was called off on January 6, 1980.[6] Even if exaggerated, these figures show that the Burmese military was willing to accept heavy casualties in order to make territorial gains against the insurgents.

The year 1979 also saw heavy fighting in the Pokaung range, near Minbu, in Sagaing Division. The local commander, Thet Tun, surrendered in the following year, along with CPB remnants in nearby Arakan State. The CPB now had only its own base area, minus Mawhpa, plus a few stragglers who were still holding out in Tenasserim Division, where a handful of guerrillas had been fighting since the outbreak of the armed struggle in 1948. The CPB now organized its "Northern

---

[4]Ibid., November 26, 1976.

[5]ကိုယ့် ၃းကိုယ်ချွန် အဆင်:ရဲ အပင်ပန်:ခံ လုံးပမ် တိုက်နိုက်တဲ့ ၄၈–၄၉ စိတ်ဓာတ်တွေ ကို မွေးြပုကြ ('The Spirit of 1948–1949 was one of self-reliance and enduring hardships"), the CPB's printing press, Panghsang, August 1979.

[6]Interview with Khin Maung Gyi, Panghsang, December 28, 1986.

Bureau" to coordinate the activities of the areas in northern Shan State and in Kachin State. The central areas around Loi Tsang became "the Central Bureau."

In 1980, the military government in Rangoon unexpectedly announced a general amnesty for all insurgents in the country. Though it was the first move of its kind since the 1963 peace talks, the response from the rebels was even less enthusiastic than before. Officially, 450 rebels from the CPB accepted the offer, along with 400 from the KIA, 260 from the Karen rebel army, 160 from "Kokang," and over 450 "expatriates." Although this adds up to 1,720, the government claimed 2,257 rebels had surrendered.[7] There is no way to cross-check these contradictory figures, but this writer is aware of surrenders only among the "Kokang group" (i.e., followers of the old opium warlord Lo Hsing-han who had been staying in the Thai border areas since he was jailed in 1973), "expatriates" (i.e., the non-Communist Burman opposition, previously led by U Nu), and the CPB remnants in the Pokaung range and Arakan State. There were no surrenders in Kachin State, and almost none among other ethnic rebels in the country or from the CPB's northeastern base area. A more realistic estimate of people who accepted the amnesty would be 600–700.

Nonetheless, both the CPB and the KIA entered into peace talks with the government during 1980. The Kachins held several rounds of talks with the régime, both in Kachin State and in Rangoon, between August 1980 and May 1981. While in Rangoon, Kachin rebel leader, Brang Seng declared that his troops were willing to lay down arms if the government granted autonomy to Kachin State, stressing that separation was no longer an issue.[8] But the rebels were offered "rehabilitation" only—no political concessions were forthcoming, and the talks eventually broke down.

In contrast, talks in May 1981 between government officials and the Communists lasted only one day. A three-man delegation, led by Thakin Pe Tint along with Ye Tun (a veteran from Pyinmana) and Hpalang Gam Di (one of Naw Seng's men), went to Lashio and put forth three demands:

1) recognition of the CPB as a legal political party;
2) recognition of the CPB's base area as an "autonomous entity";
3) recognition of the CPB's army.[9]

Apparently finding no room to negotiate, the Burmese officials ended the talks without further discussion.

After the failure of the peace talks, the CPB once again made a few feeble attempts to re-enter Burma proper. In early 1981, party veteran Bo Kyaw Moe, weary of their long confinement in the Sino-Burmese border areas, established "Force 180," with which he tried to regain a foothold in the Pinlebu area of northern Sagaing Division. The force did manage to reach Pinlebu, but was wiped out by government troops there. Bo Kyaw Moe himself was among those killed in the fighting. A second attempt was made in February 1983 by a new unit, "Force 102." Guided by the KIA, it came down from the CPB's 101 War Zone in the Kambaiti

---

[7] *Working People's Daily*, May 10, 1989.

[8] Interview with Brang Seng, Pa Jau, August 12, 1986. The *Working People's Daily* of May 10, 1989, however, claims that "the KIA held firm to the right to secede"—but this statement is not supported by meeting documents and independent sources.

[9] Interview with Ye Tun, Panghsang, December 31, 1986.

area in Kachin State and moved on towards Sagaing Division. But it was detected by the government before it reached its goal, and the troops were forced to retreat to Möng Ko in 1985. Only a small group of eighteen soldiers ventured further down to Sagaing Division, where they were pursued by government troops and forced to retreat westwards across the Chindwin river. The CPB unit remained in the Naga Hills for several months before it was able to retreat to Möng Ko as well. A separate attempt was made in 1983, when a group of "surveyors" managed to visit the old Pegu Yoma stronghold. But finding the area unsuitable for a new base area—the entire civilian population of the mountain range had been resettled in the Burmese central plain after 1975—they returned to the northeast. Since then, no attempts were made to re-enter any of the old strongholds. The CPB thus found itself isolated in the wild and remote hills along the Chinese frontier—far away from the Irrawaddy plain and Burma proper, where the party's future would have to be if its revolution was ever going to succeed.

Within the "new" CPB that had emerged in the isolated northeastern base area, there were six different groups of people with differing roots, motivations, and political backgrounds:

1) *The Sichuan lao pings,* or "the Sichuan veterans." These were the CPB cadres who had gone to China in the early 1950s and received political training there, or, in a few cases, in the Soviet Union. Because of its crucial role in setting up the northeastern base area—and its historically close links with China—this group became the most dominant even though it was numerically small. Only 143 CPB cadres had trekked to China during the period 1950–1953. They included the chairman, Thakin Ba Thein Tin; secretary, Khin Maung Gyi; the powerful political commissar of "the Northeastern War Zone," Soe Thein; the chief of staff of the CPB's "people's army," Tin Yee; and nearly half of the Central Committee.

2) *"The Old Comrades"* were the party veterans who had not gone to China, but had remained in the old base areas until these were taken over by the Burmese Army in the mid-1970s, when they joined their colleagues in the northeast. This group included Pegu Yoma veterans Myo Myint and Taik Aung, Kyaw Mya from Arakan State, and Ye Tun and Mya Min from Pyinmana. They became the second most important group in the party, next to the *Sichuan lao pings,* and they were about equally strong in numbers.

3) *The Guizhou lao pings,* or "the Guizhuo veterans," was the name given to Naw Seng's 200–300 Kachins who had spent 1950–1968 in China's Guizhuo province. During this period, the *Sichuan lao pings* were, generally speaking, the political commissars of the CPB when the northeastern base area was established in 1968–1974, and the *Guizhuo lao pings* were the military commanders. By the early 1980s many of them had become too old to lead any military operations, and they were given posts as civil administrators in various parts of the CPB's northeastern base area. Only two *Guizhuo lao pings,* Zau Mai and Hpalang Gam Di, were given prominent posts in the party leadership.

4) *"Intellectuals and newcomers."* When anti-government demonstrations swept Rangoon and Mandalay in the mid-1970s, the CPB by and large failed to link up with the anti-government movement. But approximately 150 young Burmans, mostly students, did go to the CPB's northeastern base area during the period 1974–1978. In addition, a famous ex-brigadier-general of the Burmese Army, Kyaw Zaw, defected to the CPB in 1976 along with his family. The old guard never fully trusted these new arrivals, since from the very beginning they had different views

Guizhou lao pings in China in the 1950s.
Front row, left to right: Zau Mai, Naw Seng, Hpalang Gam Di.
Photo: CPB Archives

Panghsai, November 1986. Border bridge where the Burma
Road crosses into China. Photo: Hseng Noung Lintner.

Kokang, December 1986. Photo: Bertil Lintner.

on Burmese society and politics. The "Newcomers" were considerably less orthodox and more open to new ideas and influences than either the *Sichuan lao pings* or the "Old Comrades." The suggestion that these intellectuals constituted a "pro-Soviet" faction within the party should, however, be discarded: their sympathies definitely lay with China, but in a less dogmatic way. None of the newcomers, except for Kyaw Zaw who was too famous to be ignored, were given any prominent post within the party or the army. Most of them served as office staff and medics, or were attached to heavy arms units, as they were better suited to handle mortars and recoilless rifles than were the largely illiterate Wa. The CPB's official line was that the revolution had to be led by the proletariat in alliance with the peasantry. Hence the intellectuals, despite their skills, were not considered important. Many of the ex-students had experience in, for instance, printing and writing leaflets and underground magazines. But, in accordance with official party politics, the printing press in Panghsang was managed by a former water buffalo herdsman with no previous publishing experience. He belonged, however, to "the right class" to quote the CPB's official rhetoric.

5) *Chinese volunteers.* During the period 1968–1973, "volunteers" from China in fact made up the bulk of the CPB's fighting force in the northeast; for this reason, the push into Shan State during that time was sometimes referred to as a "Red Chinese invasion." Most of these volunteers were very young; they were Red Guards of the Cultural Revolution, or Chinese youths who simply saw service with the CPB as a more exciting alternative to life in a Chinese commune. But there were also older, more experienced Chinese military advisers attached to all major CPB units until the late 1970s. In 1979, China withdrew its advisers and called back the volunteers, although a handful—who had become almost "Burmanized"—decided to remain. Among them were Zhang Zhi Ming, the commander of the 2nd Brigade at Möng Paw and one of the CPB's ablest fighters; Li Ziru of the 683 Brigade; and Lin Ming Xian, the commander of the 815 region near Laos. It is reasonable to assume that at least some of these "volunteers" were left behind by the Chinese for intelligence purposes.

6) *The national minorities.* These were the recruits drafted by the CPB in its northeastern base area. Few, if any, joined the army voluntarily; only a handful ever became party members. But they made up the entire rank-and-file of the CPB army, with the exception of the intellectuals in the artillery units. Most of the field commanders also came from the ethnic minority groups. More than two-thirds of the CPB's fighting force were Wa and the remainder Kachin, Kokang Chinese, Shan, Lahu, Akha, and others. Ethnicity and not ideology was the driving force that motivated these recruits to fight against the government. Communist literature, published by the top leadership for distribution among the rank-and-file, was willingly accepted only because the thin pages provided the troops with paper with which to roll cigarettes; in any case, since these pamphlets were written in Burmese, almost none of the private soldiers was able to read them. The only minority cadre in the top political leadership was a Shan, Sai Aung Win. He, however, did not come from the northeastern base area but was a former vice chairman of the Rangoon University Students' Union who had joined the party in the Irrawaddy Delta region in 1964.

As the years went by, some of the old leaders dropped out of the picture. Hardliner Taik Aung became paralyzed after suffering a stroke in 1983 and went to China. Thakin Pe Tint got throat cancer and had to be hospitalized in China.

Hpalang Gam Di, because of old age and ill health, also spent more and more time in Chinese hospitals. Than Shwe, the first political commissar of the northeastern base area, quit the CPB in 1985 and retired in China because of disagreements with the party leadership; he had argued that the time was not ripe for armed struggle and that it would be better, at least for the time being, to work within the present power structure in Burma.

In order to restructure the CPB, a Third Party Congress was convened at Panghsang on September 9, 1985. It lasted until October 2, and was attended by more than 170 delegates from various parts of the northeastern base area, as well as by one representative from Tenasserim, and two sympathizers from Rangoon. A new Central Committee was elected (see Appendix I) and, officially, "taking the integration of Marxism-Leninism, Mao Zedong thought with the concrete practice of Burma as guidance, the 24 day congress was a congress of unity, a congress of victory."[10]

In reality, the serious disagreements that surfaced during the congress revealed a wide generational gap between the old CPB veterans and the younger intellectuals. The Central Committee's report stated that on January 4, 1948 "Burma became a semi-colonial and semi-feudal state which is politically independent but economically dependent upon various imperialist countries. Hence, the nature of the revolution in Burma is the people's democratic revolution aimed at overthrowing imperialism, feudalism and bureaucratic capitalism." Therefore, "the tactical line for the present stage of the revolution [is that] armed struggle is the main form of struggle . . . [with the aim of] establishing bases in the rural areas surrounding the cities."[11]

This statement was criticized by the younger cadres who argued that feudal lords and greedy money lenders had passed into history long ago and that the old leaders were describing a society they had left more than thirty-five years before for the jungle, or for China. The opposition also argued that the main problems now facing the peasantry were how to meet often unrealistic production quotas set by the government, and how to avoid selling rice to the government at rates well below market prices. The same critics also questioned the use of the terms "semi-colonial" and "semi-feudal" to describe Burma and its xenophobic, atavistic régime. Rangoon's quest for self-reliance and its desire to keep outside influences—and outside trade—at an absolute minimum had created one of Asia's most thriving black-market economies on which many government servants and army officers had made fortunes. According to the younger cadres, it would be more appropriate to expose these things than to talk about "colonial exploitation." However, the opposition was defeated and some of the younger cadres were even warned not to raise such issues, or they would face disciplinary action.

But other, more serious frictions were also surfacing. The rank-and-file of the CPB army was becoming increasingly dissatisfied with the way the party leadership viewed them as little more than dispensable cannon fodder. According to the CPB's own statistics collected in 1986, there were 263,029 people in the Communist-controlled portion of Burma's Wa Hills, from which the CPB had drafted most of its recruits. Of the total, 122,399 were male and 140,630 female. Although the large disparity in numbers between the sexes—18,231—could not be attributed to war casualties alone, it nevertheless was a clear indication of the heavy toll the fight-

---

[10]*News Release, The People's Voice of Burma, the Organ of the Communist Party of Burma,* Panghsang, April 20, 1986.

[11]Ibid.

ing had taken. The CPB had imitated the Chinese tactics of using human waves when attacking an enemy position—with the result that there were few able-bodied men left in the sparsely populated Wa Hills. Because of the cut-back in aid from China, the CPB was no longer in a position to equip its troops as before; it had become a rag-tag army, whose ranks had dwindled from a peak of 23,000 regulars in 1977 to about 10,000 in 1987, plus possibly 5,000 poorly organized "village militiamen." A mutiny almost broke out in 1984, when a group of local, tribal commanders planned to capture Möng Ko and oust the old leadership of the "Northern Bureau." But the attempt was stopped by some other local commanders there, who claimed that the time was not yet ripe for an uprising against the old party leadership. However, the contradictions became sharper, and when this writer trekked through the CPB's base area for six months in 1986–1987, many private soldiers were openly talking about "taking action against the Red Burmans." There was no sympathy for Communist ideology as such; the tribal troops only made a distinction between "the Red Burmans" (i.e. the CPB's leadership) and the "the White Burmans" (the government's troops)—and they appeared equally resentful of both types of "Burmans."

THE 1989 MUTINY

The events which led to the mutiny in 1989 originated in the Chinese decision ten years earlier drastically to reduce aid to the CPB. The party's annual budget totaled Kyats 56 million in the late 1970s.[1] An official CPB breakdown shows that 67 percent of this amount came from trade (i.e., taxation of the cross-border trade with China), 25 percent from "the center" (Chinese aid); 4 percent from "the districts" (house tax on people living in the base area); 1 percent from contributions made by army personnel; and 2 percent from other unspecified sources.[2] When the Chinese decided that the CPB had to be "self-reliant," they directed all cross-border trade through Communist-controlled toll gates along the Sino-Burmese frontier. The most important was Panghsai (or Kyu-hkok) where the Burma Road crosses the international frontier into the Chinese town of Wanting. Tax levied by the CPB at Panghsai amounted to Kyats 27 million, or nearly 50 percent of the CPB's budget in the late 1970s. Black-marketeers from government-controlled areas, as well as other rebel groups (for instance the KIA, which at this time also traded in Chinese-made consumer goods), had no choice but to trade through the CPB.

In 1980, however, China announced a new open-door trade policy, and soon there were about seventy unofficially approved "gates" along the border through which Chinese goods entered Burma. The KIA could now trade directly with China; in addition some goods crossed the frontier at the only point then controlled by the government: a narrow corridor from Nongkhang in Burma to Man Khun in China, between the two CPB-controlled enclaves of Khun Hai and Man Hio opposite Namkham on the Shweli river. The government had access to a small stretch of the border opposite Muse as well, but that area was considered too insecure because of the proximity of the CPB garrison at Panghsai only a few kilometers to the east.

The Communists found it increasingly difficult to practice this new policy of "self-reliance"; due to the reduction of revenue on the cross-border trade, they turned their attention to the few resources available to them in the northeastern base area. Unlike the KIA's territory in Kachin State where the soil is rich with jade, rubies, and sapphires, there are almost no minerals in Kokang, the Wa Hills, and other CPB areas. The only cash crops were tea in Kokang—and plenty of opium

---

[1] Interview with Soe Thein, political commissar of the Northeastern base area, Panghsang, January 5, 1987.

[2] တပါတီလုံး၊ သွေး:စည်း:ညီညွတ်ပြီ: အောင်ပွဲ အရယူ ရေ: အတွက် ချီတက် ကြပါရို့ ("The Entire Party! Unite and March to Achieve Victory!") Political report of the politbureau of the CPB, submitted by Chairman Thakin Ba Thein Tin on November 1, 1978. The CPB's printing press, Panghsang, September 13, 1979, pp. 104–5.

in Kokang, the Wa Hills, and the 815 region near Laos. An estimated 80 percent of all poppy fields in Burma were already under the CPB's control, but party policy until the late 1970s had been to curb the production. With Chinese assistance, new varieties of wheat had been introduced, but few among the hill-tribe population knew how to prepare these new crops. The CPB's crop-substitution efforts ended in 1976, after an invasion of rats in the southern Wa Hills which wiped out much of the area's crops. The CPB assisted the famine victims by distributing 60,000 Indian silver rupees (still the most commonly used hard currency in the Wa Hills) and 1,600 kilograms of opium. When the crisis was over, many families had reverted to growing poppies, which are less vulnerable to pests than the substitute crops. With the reduction of Chinese aid in 1979, there was naturally even less incentive for the CPB to pursue its crop-substitution program.

The CPB now began showing increased interest in the potentially lucrative drug trade—certainly an unorthodox alternative for a party claiming to be Communist. Some leaders objected, but they were overruled by strongman Taik Aung, who at that time pulled the strings from behind the old leadership. He was determined to expand the CPB's influence over the Golden Triangle opium trade. Thousands of *viss* (1.6 kilograms) of opium were stockpiled at Panghsang. From there the party transported the drugs via Möng Pawk, in the CPB's Northern Kengtung District, to the bank of the Nam Hka river, then on by bamboo raft down to the junction of the Salween and downriver to Ta-Kaw. There it was loaded onto mules and porters and carried to the Thai border via Möng Pu-awn and Möng Hkok. Thus, the CPB became directly involved with remnants of the Kuomintang—and drug kingpin Chang Chifu alias Khun Sa—who were based along the Thai-Burmese border, where they refined the opium into heroin. The CPB also allowed increasing numbers of heroin refineries to operate within its own base area. These refineries were run by the same syndicates as the ones along the Thai border, and they had to pay "protection fees" and other taxes to the CPB. Such refineries soon were established at Pang Hpeung near Panghsang, at Wan Ho-tao in Northern Kengtung District, and near the Salween river in the Kokang area.

The CPB's official policy was confined to collecting 20 percent of the opium harvested in its base area. This opium was stockpiled at local district offices, where the CPB's "trade and commerce departments" sold it to traders from Tang-yan, Nawng Leng, Lashio, and other opium-trading centers in the government-controlled area west of the Salween. In addition, there were a 10 percent "trade tax" on opium that was sold in the local markets and a 5 percent tax on any quantity leaving the CPB's area for other destinations.[3] The funds derived from these sources were viewed as legitimate—but several local commanders became increasingly involved in other private trading activities as well as the production of heroin.

At the same time the CPB's once rather efficient civil administration began to break down. Schools and clinics had to close because of lack of funds, and party cadres showed less motivation for their work. The main preoccupation of the civil administrators out in the districts became tax collection for the party; they also engaged in trade in order to support themselves and their families. Ironically, the area controlled by the orthodox Marxist-Leninists of the CPB became a haven for

---

[3]Interview with Mya Thaung, political commissar of the Northern Wa District, Möng Mau, December 4, 1986.

free trade in then socialist Burma. The economy remained thoroughly capitalistic, and the CPB never even tried to implement a land reform in the northeast—in sharp contrast to the dramatic land-distribution schemes which the party had carried out in central Burma in the early 1950s. Communist ideology became a hollow concept without any real meaning to the people in the northeastern base areas.

Despite the strength of the CPB army, the actual party organization remained weak. In 1977, there were only 2,379 party members in Namkham, Kutkai, Kokang, Northern Wa, Southern Wa, Panghsang, and Northern Kengtung districts of whom, significantly, only 888 came from the then 23,000-strong army. In addition, there were 115 party members in Tenasserim and 26 in the central "108 War Zone." The party's youth organization claimed a membership of 2,315 and various "peasant unions"—the basis of the CPB's "people-power" structure in the northeast—enlisted 87,608 members in 882 different local organizations.[4] But these "mass organizations" existed only on paper. By the mid-1980s, the CPB had in effect ceased to function as a properly organized Communist party.

Shortly after its Third Congress in 1985, the CPB decided to launch a "rectification campaign" with the aim of "improving discipline and political as well as military training of soldiers and cadres, rebuilding the civil administration, improving relations with other rebel armies and punish [*sic*] cadres involved in illegal activites."[5] In directives related to the last item, the CPB said that any party member found to be involved in private opium trading would face severe punishment and anyone caught with 2 kilograms or more of heroin would face execution. The CPB's involvement in the drug trade had become an embarrassment to the party's aging, ideologically motivated leadership. It is also plausible to assume that the "campaign" had been launched under Chinese pressure. The spillover of drugs from the CPB's area into China was becoming a problem, and increasing amounts were also being smuggled via Kunming to Hongkong. Subsequent to the decision in 1985 to clamp down on the drug trade, party agents were sent out to check up on local cadres and report any wrong-doing to the center at Panghsang. While this did not affect the illiterate rank-and-file of the CPB, it nevertheless caused severe frictions between the top party leadership and several local commanders who had begun to act as warlords in their respective areas.

In addition, another, separate development had a tremendous impact on the rank-and-file as well as the hill-tribe population in the areas under the CPB's control. In April 1985 a delegation from the non-Communist umbrella organization, the National Democratic Front (NDF), which then comprised nine different ethnic resistance armies, left the Thai border for a long trek north. After an arduous seven-month journey, the NDF delegates reached Pa Jau, the headquarters of the Kachin rebels in the far north of the country. A meeting was held at Pa Jau, and the NDF decided to discard separatism once and for all in favor of advocating a federal system of government in Burma, and, in a significant break from past policies, they also decided to contact the CPB in order to coordinate military operations against the government in Rangoon. From Pa Jau the delegation proceeded to Panghsang, where a second meeting was held on March 17–24, 1986. The NDF and the CPB

---

[4] "The Entire Party!" p. 104.

[5] Interview with Soe Thein, Panghsang, January 5, 1987.

Third Party Congress, Panghsang, 1985. Photo: CPB Archives.

The CPB attacks Hsi-Hsinwan, November 16, 1986. Far right (with microphone), Kyi Nyint, CPB commander. Photo: Bertil Lintner.

decided to set up a united front, modeled after the anti-Vietnamese coalition in Kampuchea.[6]

Despite a great deal of initial enthusiasm, surprisingly little came out of this agreement, mainly because the pact was opposed by the second largest member of the NDF, the staunchly anti-Communist Karen National Union, which refused to cooperate with the CPB under any circumstances. But the impact of the meeting was immediately felt in the CPB's base area. The NDF delegation trekked through Möng Ko, Kokang, and over the Wa Hills before they eventually reached Panghsang. For the first time, the various ethnic minorities in the CPB's base area came into direct contact with leaders and troops from non-Communist ethnic resistance armies. The NDF delegation also included a young representative from the Wa National Army (WNA). His name was Khun Ai—and almost overnight he became somewhat of a national hero in the Wa Hills, which he had left years before to study in Rangoon, well before the CPB occupation. In what was possibly a naive attempt to placate the increasingly restless Wa, the CPB allowed the WNA to set up a liaison post at Kang Hsö inside the base area in the northern Wa Hills. But the outcome was that several of the rank-and-file CPB soldiers began wearing WNA caps and badges. The first signs of an ethnic consciousness now appeared among the Wa in the CPB's area—in contrast with the Marxist-Leninist ideology with which they had been fed for years.

The disillusionment with the old leadership increased after a series of military defeats during the 1986–1987 dry season. On November 16, 1986, the CPB attacked a government outpost on Hsi-Hsinwan mountain between Möng Paw and Panghsai. Nearly 1,000 CPB troops were mobilized for the operation, the largest the CPB had mounted in many years. The attack was launched partly because government troops had been able to disrupt the lucrative trade route to Panghsai from their mountaintop positions. But another motive was that, with the NDF becoming popular even in the CPB's own base area, the Communists were losing momentum; they wanted to show the smaller, ethnic rebel groups that they were still the strongest force and the only one able to launch a spectacular attack on a major Burmese Army camp. The Chinese no doubt supported the CPB, at least during the initial stages of the fighting, since they were also suffering from the slackening trade to Panghsai.[7]

The outpost was overrun—but only to provoke a determined counteroffensive from the Burmese Army. Thousands of troops supported by heavy artillery and aircraft, moved in on Hsi-Hsinwan. The CPB was forced to evacuate the mountain on December 7, and on January 3, 1987 the government forces pushed down from Hsi-Hsinwan and captured Möng Paw. The onslaught continued with a massive attack along the Burma Road. Panghsai fell on January 6.[8] When the threat posed by the CPB forces in this strategic border town had been removed, the government's troops crossed the Shweli river on January 13 and recaptured Khun Hai and Man Hio. At that point, persistent reports claim that China allowed the Burmese troops to use its territory to attack these two enclaves—which would indicate that the Chinese had simply decided to side with the force they thought was going to win the battle for the border area. From then onwards, the government controlled a 60-kilometer

---

[6]*Far Eastern Economic Review*, May 26, 1987.

[7]According to observations by the author at Hsi-Hsinwan, November 1986.

[8]*Far Eastern Economic Review*, February 19, 1987.

long stretch of the border, from Namkham to Panghsai, and official surface trade between Burma and China was reestablished.

In terms of actual territory, the government's gains were small, while, according to all independent sources, the price it had to pay for the victory was enormous. Goverment losses were estimated at at least 1,000 dead and wounded. But it was, nevertheless, a major victory over the CPB both strategically and in terms of prestige. The Communists had lost their most important toll gate along the border with China; financially, the CPB had suffered another setback, and the morale of its army was shattered. The CPB had used disastrous human-wave tactics, resulting in at least 200 deaths.[9] Resentment towards the old leadership became even more intense than before.

In the following year, anti-government demonstrations shook nearly every town and city throughout Burma. More than a million people marched in Rangoon and several hundred thousand in Mandalay, Moulmein, and Bassein, demanding the resignation of Burma's military régime and the restoration of democracy. The CPB paid minimal attention to the uprising. The Third Party Congress in 1985 had reiterated the Maoist doctrine of capturing the countryside first, then surrounding the cities and moving into urban areas later. Anything else was considered "adventuristic" and not in accordance with "Marxism-Leninism, Mao Zedong thought."

On May 19 and 20, 1988 the CPB's clandestine radio station, the *People's Voice of Burma*, had carried a surprisingly accurate account, apparently based on an eye-witness report, of the first anti-government demonstrations in March.[10] But that was almost the extent of the CPB's "involvement" in the pro-democracy movement in Burma of 1988.

The policy of the CPB's leadership towards the popular, nationwide uprising for democracy was, however, discussed at a Politbureau meeting at Möng Ko on September 10. Apparently, some of the party's younger members were encouraged by the urban rising and wanted to link up with it. But after discussing in general terms the movement's demand for the formation of an interim government in Rangoon, the aging Burmese Maoists concluded: "The No. 1 point I would like to say is not to let them [i.e., the younger cadres] lose sight of the fact that we are fighting a longterm war. It is impossible for us to make attacks in the towns taking months and years. That is possible only in our rural areas."[11]

In accordance with this line, the CPB launched an all-out attack on Möng Yang, a small, remote garrison town near the Chinese frontier in eastern Shan State. The CPB's forces managed to capture the town on September 24, and the commanding officer of the Burmese Army's 11th Battalion, Major Soe Lwin, was killed in the battle along with 130 of his men. At least 100 government soldiers were wounded and nine were captured alive. The government forces, however, immediately

---

[9]These are estimates made by the author while at the battlefront in northeastern Shan State from November 1986 to January 1987. Predictably, the Burmese government has released completely different figures.

[10]SWB, FE/0164B/1, May 30, 1988. The same account was also published as a booklet (in Burmese) by the CPB's printing press in Panghsang.

[11]*The Working People's Daily*, November 20, 1989. A transcript of the entire discussion was published in *the Working People's Daily* of November 18, 19, 20, and 21, 1989. Surprisingly, the government published this in order to prove that the CPB was behind Burma's pro-democracy movement.

launched a counteroffensive and on two consecutive days aircraft strafed and bombarded the town, reducing parts of it to rubble. After a few days of heavy fighting, the CPB's troops withdrew from Möng Yang.[12] The battle for Möng Yang was the CPB's last major engagement with the Burmese Army before the mutiny.

When large numbers of students fled Rangoon and other cities after the military takeover on September 18, thousands arrived in areas controlled by various members of the NDF along the Thai border and in Kachin State: significantly, only 50 to 60 went to the CPB's territory.[13] The CPB's failure to link up with the biggest popular uprising in modern Burmese history annoyed the intellectuals within the party, as well as some of the better-educated, Burmese-speaking minority cadres who had heard about the uprising in central Burma on the BBC's Burmese service. The vast majority of the CPB's hill-tribe rank-and-file was, however, unaware of the fact that there was a mass uprising in the first place.

Frictions within the CPB intensified and, all factors combined, they reached a climax by the beginning of 1989. By this time, the Chinese had signed several trade agreements with the Burmese authorities, and Chinese pressure on the CPB to reconsider its old policies was becoming more persistent. Already in 1981, the Chinese had begun offering asylum to party leaders and high-ranking cadres. This offer included a modest government pension (Rmb 250 a month for a Politbureau member; Rmb 200 for a member of the Central Committee; Rmb 180 for any other leading cadre; and Rmb 100 for ordinary party members), a house and a plot of land, on the condition that the retired CPB cadres refrained from political activity of any kind in China. The old guard, especially the *Sichuan lao pings* who had lived in China during the days of the Cultural Revolution and been close to Mao Zedong, saw the offer as treachery, although they never criticized China openly. The offer was repeated in 1985 and again in 1988. Some of the younger, lower-ranking CPB cadres accepted the offer, but none of the top party leadership did so with the exception of Than Shwe who went to China in 1985.

In early 1989, the Chinese once again approached the CPB and tried to persuade the leadership to give up and retire in China. A crisis meeting was convened on February 20 at Panghsang. For the first time Thakin Ba Thein Tin lashed out against the Chinese. In an address to the secret meeting he referred to "misunderstandings in our relations with a sister party. Even if there are differences between us, we have to coexist and adhere to the principle of noninterference in each other's affairs. This is the same as in 1981, 1985 and 1988. *We* have no desire to become revisionists."[14]

The minutes of the secret meeting were leaked, however, and this may have encouraged the disgruntled rank-and-file to rise up against the old leadership. A major reason why the mutiny did not happen earlier was that the ordinary soldiers and local commanders were uncertain of China's reaction to such a move. After all, the CPB leaders still went to China every now and then—and they were always

---

[12]Bertil Lintner, *Outrage—Burma's Struggle for Democracy* (Hongkong: Review Publishing, 1989), pp. 203–4.

[13]According to correspondence which the author received from Panghsang in April 1989.

[14]Hand-written minutes from this meeting were passed on to the author during a visit to Jinghong, Yunnan, China, in May 1989.

picked up at the border by Chinese officials in limousines; the complexities of regional politics were beyond the comprehension of most CPB soldiers.[15]

On March 12, Kokang Chinese units led by Pheung Kya-shin took the first step and openly challenged the CPB's central leadership. Two days later, his forces captured Möng Ko. The mutiny quickly spread to all other CPB base areas in the northeast. Then, late at night on April 16, troops from the predominantly Wa 12th brigade stormed Panghsang and drove the old leadership into exile in China. The radio station was also taken over, and on April 18 the mutineers broadcast the first denouncement of what they termed "the narrow racial policies of the Communist Party of Burma."[16]

An even stronger broadcast followed on April 28. The mutineers declaimed:

Conditions were good before 1979. But what has the situation come to now? No progress whatsoever is being made. Why? In our opinion, it is because some leaders are clinging to power and are obstinately pursuing an erroneous line. They are divorced from reality, practising individualism and sectarianism, failing to study and analyse local and foreign conditions, and ignoring actual material conditions. . . . They have cheated the people of the Wa region, and through lies and propaganda have dragged us into their sham revolution. . . . How can an enemy armed with modern weapons be defeated by an empty ideology and through military methods that do not integrate theory with practice? We, the people of the Wa region, never kowtow before an aggressor army whether it be local or foreign. Although we are very poor and backward in terms of culture and literature, we are very strong in our determination. What became of the lives of people in the Wa region following the wresting of power by an evil-minded individual within the CPB at a certain time in the past? It was hard life for the people. The burden on the people became heavier with more taxes being levied. We faced grave hardships. Can the people avoid staging an uprising under such a condition?[17]

It is uncertain who that "evil-minded individual" is. But while all of the most important CPB leaders escaped to China unharmed, two especially disliked figures were captured alive: Mya Thaung, the political commissar of Northern Wa District, and Soe Thein, the overall political commissar of the Northeastern Region, who was notorious for manipulating the ethnic minorities. A third high-ranking CPB member who was earmarked for arrest—and possible execution—was the chief of staff of the army, Tin Yee, who in the past had been responsible for sending many young Wa to die in human-wave attacks on government positions. But Tin Yee swam across the Nam Hka river the night the 12th Brigade attacked, and escaped to China with the other top leaders from Panghsang.

Within a month of the initial uprising in Kokang, the CPB ceased to exist—almost 50 years after its formation in the flat in Rangoon's Barr Street, and 41 years since it decided to resort to armed struggle against the government.

---

[15] According to numerous conversations between CPB soldiers overheard by the author during a visit to the CPB's base area from November 1986 to April 1987.

[16] SWB, FE/0439B/1, April 20, 1989.

[17] FBIS-EAS-89-081, April 28, 1989.

SOME CONCLUDING OBSERVATIONS

The 1989 mutiny within the CPB not only altered the military map of Burma and opened possibilities for new alliances in the country's decades-long civil war. Perhaps even more importantly, it put the ruling military in Rangoon in a dilemma, since it removed the "Communist specter" in Burmese politics which for more than two decades has been the army's justification for perpetuating its dominant position in the government and Burmese society.

Given the diverse ethnic composition of the CPB and the fact that Communist ideology—which had been its former unifying factor, however weak—it is hardly surprising that attempts to keep the various units together under one umbrella failed almost immediately. By the end of 1989, the former CPB had broken up into a number of smaller groups:

People's Liberation Front (PLF) (ပြည်သူ့ လွတ်မြောက်ရေး တပ်ဦး:) is the new name for the local unit in Kachin State, formerly known as the 101 War Zone. Given its ethnic cohesiveness—all its cadres, troops, and two most important leaders, Ting Ying and Zalum, are Kachin—the PLF has had fewer internal problems than the other factions. The PLF forged an alliance with the KIA and, by the end of 1989, it had in effect rejoined the "mother army" from which it originally split in 1969.

The Burma National Democratic Alliance Army (BNDAA) (မြန်မာပြည် အမျိုးသား ဒီမိုကရေစီ မဟာမိတ် တပ်မတော်) was the name adopted by the first mutineers in Möng Ko and Kokang, led by Pheung Kya-shin, when they revolted against the CPB in mid-March 1989. Most of the followers are Kokang Chinese and Kachin, plus some Wa. Given its heavy involvement in the local opium trade, this group was from the beginning more inclined towards business than politics.

The Burma National United Party/Army (BNUP/BNUA) (မြန်မာပြည် အမျိုးသား သွေးစည်းရေး ပါတီ/တပ်မတော်) After the fall of Panghsang, the CPB's former Northern and Southern Wa Districts, plus Panghsang Special Township, combined and formed this group, headquartered at Panghsang. It established close links with the WNA and also approached the NDF for possible membership. Chao Ngi Lai was elected general secretary of the BNUP and Pao Yo Chang became the commander of the BNUA; they had been the only Wa to be admitted as alternate members of the CPB's Central Committee at the 3rd congress in 1985. Others who rallied behind the BNUP included *Guizhou lao ping* Zau Mai; Li Ziru, one of the few remaining Chinese volunteers who joined the CPB in the late 1960s; and Kyaw Htin, a Shan and former battalion commander in the CPB's army. A few of the intellectuals who joined the CPB in the 1970s also joined this group, which became the most potent

Bertil Lintner and Thakin Ba Thein Tin, Panghsang, January 1987.
Photo: Hseng Noung Lintner.

Pegu Yoma survivors Aung Sein and Than Maung, plus Aung Htet (Thakin Ba
Thein Tin's personal assistant), Panghsang. Photo: Hseng Noung Lintner.

force of the ex-CPB army. On November 3, 1989, the BNUP/BNUA merged with some non-Communist Wa forces along the Thai border and became the United Wa State Party/Army (UWSP/UWSA)—but with the leadership intact.

The Burma (Eastern Shan State) National Democratic Army (ပြည်ထောင်စု မြန်မာနိုင်ငံရှမ်းပြည်နယ် အရှေ့ပိုင်း အမျိုးသားဒီမိုကရေစီ တပ်မတော်) was set up in the former 815 Region (the Mekong River Division) in 1989 by Lin Ming Xian, another of the few Chinese volunteers who stayed behind with the CPB when the others were recalled to China in the late 1970s. His forces became a warlord army, living on smuggling timber to China and opium down to the Thai border. Lin Ming Xian is married to Pheung Kya-shin's daughter; he soon established links with the Kokang group.

Noom Suk Harn: The Shan-dominated former 768 Brigade declared its "independence" on May 15 and assumed this name. It means "the Young Brave Warriors" and was the name adopted by the first Shan rebels in the late 1950s. Its political leader was Khun Myint, and the army was led by Sai Noom Pan, the Shan ex-commander of 768, and Zhang Zhi Ming, another of the erstwhile Chinese volunteers who stayed behind in Burma. However, in-fighting soon broke out in the area and Sai Noom Pan's erstwhile deputy, a Welsh-Shan rebel commander called Sao Khun Sa alias Michael Davies, was assassinated in May 1989. A few months later, the short-lived *Noom Suk Harn* was taken over by Lin Ming Xian's forces in the former 815 Region.

The Burmese military's initial response to these unprecedented developments was confused and erratic. Since the army violently reasserted its power in Rangoon on September 18, 1988, it has tried to justify its action by referring to a supposed "CPB threat." An unusually imaginative article in the state-run *Working People's Daily* of November 12–13, 1989 was titled "BCP [the government always refers to the CPB as the BCP] fifth-columnists in the midst of slogans for democracy." It ran: "When the students had been gathered together in force, BCP hardcore students assumed positions of leadership. In no way could ordinary students with ordinary dissatisfaction match the militancy and activity of the students of the BCP cells who have been specially nurtured and prepared for such occasions of agitation and militant activities . . . and believe me, this is no speculation on my part. I know for a fact just how many underground BCP hardcore cadres have come seeping aboveground" (*sic*).

The rest of the article was in the same ranting style, without substantiation of any of the outlandish accusations. But despite the crudeness of the propaganda, the issue of the "Communist threat" has been played up not only by the Burmese military but also by some personalities in Rangoon who had initially played important roles in last year's pro-democracy movement, notably ex-Brigadier-General Aung Gyi and the local correspondent for the *Associated Press*, Sein Win. A major rift over the issue occurred in December 1988 within the largest opposition party, the National League for Democracy (NLD), of which Aung Gyi was the chairman, ex-General Tin U the vice chairman, and Aung San Suu Kyi the general secretary. Aung Gyi presented a list of eight alleged Communists in the NLD's top leadership: Ko Yu, Myint Myint Khin, Moe Thu, Win Tin, Tin Shwe, Htun Tin, Aung Lwin, and Chan Aye. Aung Gyi was asked to substantiate his allegations, or resign from his post. He left the NLD on December 3 along with twelve of his associates. The Aung Gyi faction also claimed that the septuagenarian, former member of the CPB's Central Committee, Thakin Tin Mya, had "a secret office" in the house of NLD secretary general, Aung San Suu Kyi, and acted as her "main adviser."

Other observers pointed out that Thakin Tin Mya's role in the 1988 uprising had been confined to moral support, and that only two of the eight alleged Communists in the NLD's leadership had at any stage been associated with Communist organizations. Ko Yu belonged to Thakin Soe's Red Flag faction until 1960; Chan Aye was in the CPB underground from 1948 until he was arrested in 1957. Both had denounced communism after their return to Rangoon. The other six on the list were lawyers, film actors, and writers who had never been active in the CPB or similar organizations. But the issue was kept alive to cast suspicion on the pro-democracy movement in Burma, with the apparent aim of discrediting the opposition—and to enable the army to claim that it had valid reasons for staging its bloody crackdown on dissent on September 18, 1988.

The advocates of the military's line claimed that there was "an armed, underground CPB" in the jungle, and "secret cells" and activists in the cities who masterminded opposition activities. This ran contrary to historical facts, since the CPB had already lost most of its influence in urban areas in the early 1950s when it adopted the Maoist line of building up bases in the countryside to surround the urban areas. What was left of the CPB's urban movement became defunct after the *pyouk-touk-hta* purges in the 1960s. The leftists—present or former—in Rangoon belong to a completely different tradition: they are either remnants of the legal, left-wing, trade union-based opposition that existed before the 1962 coup (mainly the BWPP and its extension in the NUF, plus the TUC[B] and the ABPO), or they are defectors from the CPB who returned mainly during the period 1957–1958.

The ex-BWPP cadres have gone in different directions since the 1962 coup. Some, such as Ba Nyein, became advisers to the new military government, as did the former CPB leader, Thakin Thein Pe (who later became known known as Thein Pe Myint). After the pseudo-coup in 1988, others set up their own political parties which to some extent are modern versions of the old BWPP: Thakin Chit Maung's Democratic Front for National Reconstruction and Thakin Lwin's People's Democratic Party. The CPB defectors—Thakin Tin Mya, Bo Ye Htut, Thakin Soe (who died in May 1989), Chan Aye, and others—were frequently referred to by the CPB leaders interviewed at Panghsang in December 1986–March 1987 as "traitors" and "renegades" who had "betrayed the revolution."

Nonetheless, the military régime continued to use the "Communist specter" for obvious political reasons. Consequently, the ruling military found it difficult to cope with the situation which emerged in the wake of the 1989 mutiny. At a press conference held in Rangoon on May 12, 1989, a military spokesman said: "There has been a split in the BCP [i.e. CPB] as a result of the Kokang group and another Wa group leaving the *main* BCP body ... this split has definitely weakened the BCP as an underground insurgent force but this might shift their destructive activities into urban areas ... there are some BCP elements in cities and towns [where] they still pose danger to some extent."[1]

---

[1]Press Release No. 11/89 from the Embassy of the Union of Burma, Bangkok, May 16, 1989, my italics.

The CPB leaders and cadres—altogether about 300 people—who had been driven out of Möng Ko and Panghsang first escaped to China, where the authorities placed them under arrest in the Yunnanese border towns of Man Hai and Meng Lien; they were hardly in a position to "shift their destructive activities" to Rangoon or any other place in Burma.

The Chinese were also faced with a dilemma when the deposed CPB leaders fled across the border on April 17. Since the late 1970s Beijing's policy had gradually shifted from all-out support for the CPB towards greater economic cooperation with whoever controlled the Sino-Burmese border areas, although the emphasis was on improving official relations with the government in Rangoon. The entire CPB leadership initially were kept with their families in the small Yunnanese border town of Meng Lien, opposite Panghsang. Those who had fled from Northern Bureau headquarters sought temporary shelter in Man Hai just across the border river in the Möng Ko valley. But in view of the improved relations between Beijing and the military government in Rangoon, the presence of the former CPB leaders in Yunnan proved an embarrassment for the Chinese authorities. At first the Chinese tried to persuade the mutineers to let their former leaders return and reside on the Burmese side of the border. But the new non-Communist leadership in Panghsang turned down the proposal, prompting the Chinese to look elsewhere for a solution.

On June 22, the ex-CPB exiled in China—including Thakin Ba Thein Tin, Khin Maung Gyi, Myo Myint, Kyin Maung, Tin Yee, and Kyaw Zaw—were transported in Chinese army vehicles through Yunnan up to Kambaiti Pass in the former 101 War Zone. The local unit there had teamed up with the KIA in the wake of the mutiny, and the Kachin rebels, under severe Chinese pressure, agreed to let the former CPB leaders stay in their area on the condition that they would not engage in any further political activities.[2] Despite this, the military continues to claim that there was still a CPB, consisting of a main force somewhere in the jungle as well as underground cells in the cities. It is clear that, for the sake of its own hold of power, the military is unwilling to admit that the CPB is defunct—both in the jungle and in urban areas.

The most extreme manifestation of the "conspiracy theory" came on August 5, 1989, when the chief of Burma's military intelligence, Brigadier-General Khin Nyunt, delivered a six-hour speech, accusing the CPB of "plotting to destabilise the government." The speech was later printed as a book and distributed widely in Burma and abroad.[3] But apart from colorful details about alleged "conspiratory meetings" by "hardcore Communist organisers" in the Coca-Cola Restaurant in Kokkine, a Rangoon suburb, Khin Nyunt's speech offered little hard evidence to substantiate the allegations. The only evidence cited to support the claim that the opposition in Rangoon were in league with the CPB were two letters, supposedly sent by the CPB to Aung San Suu Kyi and her mother, Khin Kyi, who died on December 27, 1988. The first letter had been burned, Khin Nyunt stated, adding that "it could not be said for sure whether or not the [the second] letter reached Aung San Suu Kyi."[4] The ruling élite's inability to accept the fact that the 1988 uprising was a genuine expression of popular discontent with an inept and repres-

---

[2]*Far Eastern Economic Review*, August 24, 1989.

[3]*Burma Communist Party's Conspiracy to Take over State Power* (Rangoon: News and Periodicals Enterprise, September 1989) (174 pages).

[4]Ibid., pp. 5, 7, and 53.

sive régime, and not a "conspiracy" of any kind, only exacerbated the already tense relationship between the Burmese military and the public at large.

To the surprise of many, however, Khin Nyunt's lengthy speech contained a detailed description of a plan which the CPB purportedly had drawn up "to seize state power." He went on to claim that a "4828 Regional Party Committee (Communist Party of Burma)"—named after the CPB's uprising day: March 28, 1948—had been set up to coordinate the activities of underground cells in "Lower Burma" and in "Upper Burma." Closer inspection revealed that the "4828 Committee" was not set up by the insurgent CPB; it was an attempt by some former CPB members to take advantage of the pro-democracy uprising with the final aim of forming an entirely new Communist party in Burma. The leader of the group was Thet Tun, a former political commissar of the CPB remnants in the Pokaung Range (Magwe Division), who had surrendered along with his followers during the 1980 amnesty. The group also included a few ex-CPB members who had spent the1960s and 1970s on Coco Island, a former penal colony in the Andaman Sea. The tiny band had no contact with the insurgent CPB and was little more than a historic curiosity. According to Burmese students who were contacted by the "4828 Committee" in Rangoon in September 1988, it was a fringe group whose role in the mass uprising of that year was minimal. It is uncertain whether Khin Nyunt in his speech deliberately tried to muddle the issue, or if the mix-up reflected poor intelligence work.

While the Burmese public was being fed unrealistic propaganda with regard to the CPB's activities during the 1988 uprising, along with an equally distorted version of the 1989 mutiny and its aftermath, the Burmese military authorities were also in fact negotiating secretly with some of the mutineers. The first step in that direction was taken on March 20, only a week after the first mutiny in the north, when the Northeastern Command of the Burmese Army in Lashio sent an unusual envoy to negotiate with the Kokang leader, the former "opium king" of the Golden Triangle, Lo Hsing-han. In the 1960s, Kokang-born Lo had led a local Ka Kwe Ye, or home guard, unit based in Lashio. Lo had fought alongside the Burmese Army against the CPB at the crucial battle at the Kunlong bridge in 1971–1972 and in return been given the right to use all government-controlled roads and towns in Shan State for opium smuggling.

The entire Ka Kwe Ye program was, however, abandoned in 1973 when some of the local home-guard warlords became too powerful to control. Lo was among those who did not respond to the call to surrender; instead, he went underground and briefly teamed up with the Shan rebels in the SSA. Lo was eventually arrested in Thailand on August 16, 1973 and deported to Burma where he was sentenced to death, not for opium trafficking but for "insurrection against the state." But Lo was released during the 1980 amnesty and returned to Lashio where he quietly began rebuilding his former home-guard unit.[5]

Lo Hsing-han's renewed usefulness to the Burmese military authorities was not fully recognized until the 1989 mutiny. Back in his native Kokang, Lo met Pheung Kya-shin and Pheung Kya-fu and reached an agreement, similar to the earlier one

---

[5]*The Return of Lo Hsing-han*, FOCUS magazine, Bangkok, August 1981; "An Unconventional Weapon," *Far Eastern Economic Review*, June 18, 1982. See also Lintner, *Outrage*, pp. 71 and 91. For a description of the relationship between the Burmese Army and its Ka Kwe Ye home guards, see Alfred McCoy *The Politics of Heroin in Southeast Asia* (New York: Harper, 1972), pp. 314 and 332–38, and Bertil Lintner, "The Shans and the Shan States of Burma," *Contemporary Southeast Asia* [Singapore] (March 1984).

between the Ka Kwe Ye and the Burmese Army. The warlords were given a free hand in the drug traffic, provided that they turned against the *bona fide* insurgents in the region. Heroin refineries were already in operation in the areas near Möng Ko, Möng Hom, and Hpaunghsaing.

A second outside delegation visited Kokang in April. On the 20th, a meeting was held in Lashio between Kokang representatives, Lo Hsing-han, and the politician Aung Gyi from Rangoon. Two days later, Brigadier-General Khin Nyunt and Brigadier-General Maung Thint, went to Kunlong where they met with Pheung Kya-shin's younger brother, Pheung Kya-fu. A temporary ceasefire was agreed upon. In return, the Kokang group received Kyats 5 million in "development aid" and a few thousand bags of rice. Lo, using his contacts with the Burmese Army, reportedly also assisted the mutineers in transporting the heroin out of Kokang and further on to Lashio, Mandalay, and Rangoon. An intelligence report compiled on September 9, 1989, alleged that the northeastern commander of the Burmese Army, Lashio-based Brigadier-General Maung Thint, ensured the safe passage of these convoys.[6]

A special "Central Committee for development of border areas and national races" was set up in Rangoon on May 30, headed by Lieutenant-General Than Shwe, the commander-in-chief of the Burmese Army, and including Brigadier-General Khin Nyunt and other high-ranking military officers.[7] Following the intitial success in Kokang, the committee made a second deal a few months later with the new leaders of the former 815 region. On November 11, 1989, the Wa leader Chao Ngi Lai and some of his followers were taken by helicopter from the Wa Hills to Lashio to meet Khin Nyunt and several other high-ranking Burmese Army officers.[8] Fighting along the former CPB front ceased altogether during 1989 except in Kachin State.

In theory, the mutiny could facilitate a political solution to Burma's decades-long civil war, since there now are only ethnic rebels in the country and no Communists. But, given the Rangoon régime's past record of demanding surrender of all insurgents with no willingness to concede to any political demands, it was hardly surprising that the deals made with the ex-CPB mutineers were business-oriented and did not include any provisions for regional autonomy or official peace talks. Unofficial negotiations, however, were held in Rangoon from November 16 to December 6, 1989. The ex-CPB team consisted of Pheung Kya-fu, two of his lieutenants (Liu Go Chi and Liu Go Myint), Ting Ying from the old 101 War Zone, and Zhang Zhi Ming of the former 815 Region. The former rebel commanders were promised rice, money, some development aid, and the right to maintain 1,000 men each, converted into government-supervised militia forces. In October, a few months before the secret talks in Rangoon, a high-powered Burmese military delegation had paid a 12-day visit to China. The delegation was led by Lieutenant-General Than Shwe, commander-in-chief of the Burmese Army, and included Colonel Kyaw Than, commander of the 99th Light Infantry Division, whose area of responsibility

---

[6]"Confidential Narcotics Update, 9.9.1989," from the Kachin Independence Organization. Information to the same effect was passed on to the author in private correspondence with local people in northeastern Shan State. The claim has also been supported by Western diplomats based in Rangoon.

[7]*Working People's Daily* [Rangoon], May 31, 1989.

[8]*Far Eastern Economic Review*, June 28, 1990.

covers the hills opposite Kokang and Möng Ko. This could indicate that Beijing played a behind-the-scenes role in the talks.[9]

But these negotiations were never publicized officially and no political concessions were in any case granted; intelligence sources emphasized that the deal between the government and the ex-CPB mutineers was based on business, including provisions for the trade in narcotics drugs from the area down to Rangoon, to the Thai border, and to India.

Rangoon's unwillingness to find an actual political solution to the country's civil war can be explained by the fact that the military has a vested interest in continuing the conflict. A political settlement—or a final military victory, even if that seems impossible—could involve a reduction in the army's strength to a 20,000–30,000-strong border security force, which is all that Burma would actually need.

But would the army accept such a diminished role? The answer is no, unless a group of younger, more enlightened army officers in Burma decide to stage a genuine coup against the present leadership in Rangoon. The likelihood of such a scenario is less remote today because of the removal of the "Communist threat." Seen in that perspective, the rebels in Burma's northeast might for the first time have done something which could influence Burmese national politics.

---

[9]Ibid., December 28, 1989

BIOGRAPHIES

AUNG SAN, Thakin

Born in 1915 in Natmauk, Magwe District. Key leader of the 1936 student strike in Rangoon, secretary general of the Dohbama Asiayone. One of the participants in the August 15, 1939 meeting of the Marxist study group, but he never participated in CPB activities. Left secretly for Amoy, China, in 1940 but ended up in Tokyo. Returned to Burma on a mission to gather recruits for military training in Japan. The group, known as "the Thirty Comrades," set up the Burma Independence Army (BIA) in Bangkok on December 26, 1941 and entered Burma with the Japanese soon afterwards. Minister of defense in Dr Ba Maw's puppet government in 1943, contacted the British and officially turned against the Japanese on March 27, 1945 . Negotiated Burma's independence with the British on January 27, 1947. Signed the Panglong Agreement with leaders of the Shan, Chin, and Kachin minorities on February 12. Assassinated with six of his ministers and two others on July 19, 1947. Considered the father of Burma's independence and a national hero. His daughter Aung San Suu Kyi emerged in 1988 as Burma's most prominent opposition leader.

AUNG WIN, Sai

Shan. Born in 1937 in Loi-Lem, Shan State. Vice chairman of the Rangoon University Students' Union (RUSU), 1961–1962. Participated in the July 1962 student movement against the military. Joined the CPB in January 1964 in Henzada District. Went to Shan State in 1969 and became a member of the Central Committee in 1975. Reelected during the Third Congress in 1985. In charge of the economic department at the Northern Bureau (Möng Ko) until he moved to Panghsang in April 1987. Joined the 1989 mutiny.

AYE NGWE

Sino-Burmese. Born in 1919 in Myaungmya District in the Irrawaddy Delta region. Undergraduate from Rangoon University. Joined the CPB in May 1941. Sent by the CPB to China in September 1941 to contact the Chinese Communists. Studied at the Southwest Associated University in Kunming. Participated as interpreter in the tripartite talks between the Communist Party of China (CPC), the Kuomintang, and the United States in 1945 in Chungking. Recognized as CPB representative to the CPC in 1945; went to the Jinchar-Hubei-Chachar base area in 1946 and became member of the CPC. Appointed interpreter for the CPB cadres who arrived in China in the early 1950s. Transferred from the CPC to the CPB in 1967 but resided in Beijing until 1978, when he went to Panghsang with the central office. Became an

Thakin Ba Thein Tin, the CPB's last chairman. Photo: Hseng Noung Lintner.

Chao Ngi Lai, the Wa leader who joined the mutiny. Photo: Bertil Lintner.

alternate member of the Central Committee at the Third Congress in 1985. Fled to China when the mutiny broke out in April 1989.

BA HEIN, Thakin

Born in 1913 in Mandalay. President of the All-Burma Students' Union in 1935. Translated Marxist literature for the *Nagani* Book Club in Rangoon. Leader of the Dohbama Asiayone and the leftist Freedom Bloc; organized the oil workers in Yenengyaung. One of the first *thakin* to join the CPB in 1939. Imprisoned by the British in Mandalay, 1940–1942. Served in the wartime government of Dr. Ba Maw but went underground in 1945 as a resistance leader in the Toungoo area. Became member of the Central Committee at the Second Congress in 1945. President of the All-Burma Trade Union Congress (ABTUC), 1945–1946. Editor of the *People's Power* or *Pyithu Ana* (ြပည်သူ့ အာဏာ) magazine. Died from malaria on November 20, 1946. Married to Daw Khin Gyi who attended the Second Congress of the Communist Party of India in February 1948 in Calcutta. Considered the father of "true communism" in Burma by the CPB.

BA THEIN TIN, Thakin

Born in 1914 in Tavoy; son of a Chinese petty trader and an ethnic Burman mother. Attended primary and secondary school at Tavoy, passing his matriculation exam in 1931 and gaining admittance to Rangoon University. Unable to further his studies because his debt-ridden father could not afford university fees. Became full-time worker for the Dohbama Asiayone in 1938 and joined the CPB in October 1939. District party committee organizer in Tavoy; fought against the Japanese in Tavoy in 1945. Became a member of the Central Committee at the Second Congress in 1945; member of the Politbureau in 1946. Participated in the 1947 British Empire Communist Parties Conference in London and, in February 1948, went to Calcutta together with then CPB chairman Thakin Than Tun to attend the Second Congress of the Communist Party of India. Went underground in March 1948 and was elected vice chairman of the CPB in 1950. Left for China in 1953. Attended several party congresses in Moscow and Beijing, and visited Hanoi in 1963. *De facto* leader of the CPB since the mid-1960s but did not become official party chairman until the death of Thakin Zin on March 15, 1975. Resided in China until 1978. Re-elected chairman at the Third Congress in 1985. Fled to China during the mutiny in April 1989.

CHAO NGI LAI

Wa. Born in 1939 in Kyauk Chung village, northern Wa Hills. Local warlord in the Saohin-Saohpa area, northern Wa Hills. Contacted by the CPB in 1968; captured Saohpa together with Kyaw Htin from the CPB in December 1969. Appointed commander of the 2nd Battalion of the CPB's army and became an alternate member of the Central Committee at Third Congress in 1985. One of the most important leaders of the 1989 mutiny; elected general secretary of the new Burma National United Party (BNUP) in May 1989, and general secretary of the United Wa State Party (UWSP) in November..

CHIT, Thakin

Born in 1910 in Thanatpin, Pegu District. Schoolteacher in Mandalay; joined the People's Revolutionary Party in the 1940s and later the Socialist Party. Member of the CPB in September 1946; leader of the All-Burma Trade Union Congress. Went underground in March 1948; member of the Central Committee and elected to the Politbureau in 1951. Leader of the cadres in the Pegu Yoma. Became secretary of the Central Committee after Thakin Than Tun's death in October 1968. Killed in the Pegu Yoma on March 15, 1975.

CHIT MAUNG, Thakin

Born in1915 in Tharrawaddy District. Participated in the 1936 students' strike and joined the Dohbama Asiayone in 1937. Elected MP for the AFPFL in 1947, leader of the All-Burma Peasants' Organization (ABPO) and founding member of the Burma Workers' and Peasants' Party (BWPP) in December 1950. Active in the National Unity Front (NUF) in the 1950s. Re-emerged as a leftist leader in September 1988. Now chairman of the Democratic Front for National Reconstruction.

GOSHAL H. N. (alias) Thakin Ba Tin

Burma-born Bengali. Graduated from Rangoon University; joined the CPB in 1939. Fled to India during the Japanese occupation and became member of the Communist Party of India. Returned to Burma after World War II and organized the All-Burma Trade Union Congress. Member of the Central Commitee and the Politbureau in 1946. Claimed that strikes and demonsrations rather than armed struggle would bring down the government in Rangoon, but nevertheless went underground with the CPB in March 1948. Briefly expelled from the party for advocating a peace settlement with the government. Branded "Burma's Liu Shaoqi," and executed in the Pegu Yoma on June 18, 1967.

HTAY, yebaw

Joined the CPB during World War II; became a member of the Central Committee at the Second Congress in July 1945. Initiated the "Peace and Coalition Government"-line in the 1950s; leader of the CPB's delegation to the 1963 peace talks in Rangoon. Branded "Burma's Deng Xiaoping" by the party's radical faction, and executed on July 18, 1967 in the Pegu Yoma.

KHIN MAUNG GYI

Born in 1927 in Rangoon. His father was an inspector of land records in the Rangoon Development Trust. Joined the anti-Japanese struggle in 1944 while working for the East-Asiatic Youth League. Became CPB member in late 1945. Passed 2nd MBBS at the Junior Medical College in Rangoon in 1949; executive member of the All-Burma Students' Union (ABSU). Was nominated to represent the ABSU at the International Union of Students (IUS) in Prague and tried to go to Czechsolovakia in 1950. Reached Calcutta, but had to return to Burma because of financial difficulties. Joined the CPB unit in Prome and went to China in 1953. Studied Marxism-Leninism at the Higher Party School in Beijing until 1957. Left for Moscow where he studied Marxism-Leninism, 1957–1960; attended Moscow's Academy of Social Sciences, 1961–1963; wrote thesis on agrarian problems in Burma and worked for a few months at the Institute of World Economy in Moscow. Returned to Beijing in 1963 and became Thakin Ba Thein Tin's personal secretary as well as member of the "leading group of five" set up in China in November. Visited Hanoi in 1965; attended the Fifth Congress of the Albanian Party of Labour in Tirana in 1967 along with Thakin Pe Tint. Vice political commissar of the first CPB unit that entered Burma from China on January 1, 1968. Became member of the Central Committee and the

Khin Maung Gyi, secretary to the Central Committee.
Photo: Hseng Noung Lintner.

Kyaw Mya, the CPB leader from Arakan, now in China.
Photo: Hseng Noung Lintner.

Politbureau in 1975. Second vice chairman of the CPB from 1975 to the Third Congress in 1985 when that post was abolished. In the Central Bureau, 1980–1984; returned to Panghsang to attend the Third Congress. Secretary to the Central Committee from the Third Congress until the 1989 mutiny when he fled to China. The CPB's main theoretician since the early 1960s.

KYAW MYA

Born in 1915 in Paletwa, now Arakan State. Arakanese. Entered Rangoon University in 1934 and obtained a BA in English (honors) in 1940. Worked as clerk at Kyaukpyu, Arakan, until World War II broke out. Participated in the anti-Japanese struggle; joined the CPB in 1946. District party secretary in Sittwe, 1946–1951; CPB leader of Arakan, 1951–1979. Alternate member of the Central Committee in 1955; member of the Central Committee and the Politbureau in 1975. Left Arakan for Bangladesh in 1979; flew via Dhaka and Karachi to Beijing and continued through China to Panghsang. Settled in China shortly before the 1989 mutiny.

KYAW ZAW, Bo (alias) Thakin Shwe

Born in 1919 in Saingsu, Thonze township, Tharrawaddy District. Active in the Dohbama Asiayone; one of the Thirty Comrades who went to Japan for military training in 1941. Commander of the No. 4 Military Region of the Burma National Army (BNA) in 1945. Joined the CPB in 1944 and elected member of the Central Committee at the Second Congress in July 1945 but never participated in party activities. Southern commander of the Burmese Army from independence until 1952; then northern commander and in charge of the operations against the Kuomintang in Shan State. Accused of leaking news to the CPB and forced to leave the army in 1956. Officially dismissed on June 7, 1957. Lived in retirement in Sanchaung, Rangoon, until July 1976 when he went to Man Hio and joined the CPB. Member of the Central Committee and the Central Military Commission. Vice chief of General Staff of the CPB until the 1989 mutiny when he fled to China.

KYIN MAUNG (alias) *yebaw* Tun

Born in 1924 in Sagaing. Joined the Burma Independence Army (BIA) in 1942 and the CPB in 1943. Soe Thein's cousin. Went underground in March 1948 and became vice political commissar of the CPB forces in the Kyawkku-Lawng Long-Nawng Wu area of Shan State. Member of the Central Committee and the Politbureau in 1975. Chief of propaganda and publicity. Stayed at the Northern Bureau (Möng Ko) until 1987 when he was transferred to Panghsang. Fled to China during the 1989 mutiny.

LET YA, Bo (alias) Thakin Hla Pe

Born in 1911. Active in the Dohbama Asiayone. Founding member of the CPB on August 15, 1939 but never participated in party activities. One of the Thirty Comrades. Deputy prime minister after the assassination of Aung San in July 1947. Governor's counselor for defense. Negotiated Defense Agreement with the British at Kandy in 1945. Deputy prime minister and minister for defense immediately before independence (1947–1948). Resigned from all posts in 1948 and became businessman. Joined U Nu's non-Communist resistance against the military government in the 1960s; commander of the rebel Patriotic Liberation Army (PLA) in 1969; chairman of the People's Patriotic Party (PPP) in March 1973. Killed by Karen rebels near the Thai border in November 1978.

Kyaw Zaw, ex-brigadier general of the Burmese Army who joined the CPB in 1976.
Photo: Hseng Noung Lintner.

Li Ziru, the Chinese "volunteer" who joined the mutiny.
Photo: Hseng Noung Lintner.

LI ZIRU

Chinese. Born in 1946 (?) in Baoshan in China's Yunnan province. Joined the CPB as volunteer in 1968 along with Zhang Zhi Ming and Lin Ming Xian. Attached to the CPB's "special forces" which captured Panghsai/Kyu-hkok in March 1970. Political commissar of the 4045 Battalion (under the 683 Brigade) which in accordance with the "7510 Plan" crossed the Salween River in 1975. Vice chief of staff of the Central Bureau forces in 1980; later, military commander of the Central Bureau. Became an alternate member of the Central Committee during the Third Congress in 1985. Joined the mutiny in 1989 and became one of the leaders of the Panghsang-based Burma National United Party (BNUP), now renamed the United Wa State Party (UWSP).

LWIN, Thakin

Born in 1914 in Zigon. Secretary of the Oilfield Workers' Association 1938–1941. Elected MP in 1947 and president of the Trade Union Congress (Burma) in 1949. Withdrew from U Nu's Anti-Fascist People's Freedom League (AFPFL) in 1949 and formed the leftist Burma Workers' and Peasants' Party (BWPP) in 1950. Active in the National Unity Front (NUF) in the 1950s. In retirement after the 1962 coup d'état but re-emerged as a political leader in September 1988. Chairman of the People's Democratic Party which registered on October 4, 1988.

MYINT, Khun

Shan. Born in 1930 in Möng Mang in Yunnan, China. Moved to Möng Yang, Burma's Shan State, in 1935. Educated at a Buddhist monastery. Joined the Shan rebellion and became a local commander of the Kengtung-based Shan National Army (SNA) in 1961. Based at Huey Nam Khun on the Thai border in the mid-1960s. Merged his forces with the Shan State Army (SSA) and became its eastern commander in 1971. Set up the Shan People's Liberation Army (SPLA) in 1974 and forged an alliance with the CPB. The SPLA became the CPB's 768 Brigade in August 1976. Civil administrator in the Hsaleü area east of Möng Yang although he never joined the party. Joined the 1989 mutiny.

MYO MYINT (alias) *yebaw* Aung

Born in 1924 in Letpadan, Tharrawaddy District. Active in the student and youth movement in his hometown. Joined the Burma Defense Army (BDA) in 1942; attended the Japanese-run Officers' Training School in Rangoon. Joined the CPB in 1943. Member of the Central Committee since 1948. Participated in the uprising in the Pyinmana area together with Thakin Pe Tint, 1948–1953, and became political commissar of the CPB's Third Division (southern Pegu Yoma, Pegu, and Hantha-waddy/Rangoon). Chairman of the CPB's northern region, 1953–1967. Back in the Pegu Yoma, 1967-71; attached to the Pa-O national movement in Shan State, 1971–1975; member of the Politbureau since 1975. Based at the Northern Bureau (Möng Ko), 1975–1987, and at Panghsang from 1987 until the 1989 mutiny when he fled to China.

NAAG, Dr. (alias) *yebaw* Tun Maung

Bengali. Leading Communist organizer in Burma and chief of the CPB's central medical staff. Educated the CPB's first medics.

NAW SENG

Kachin. Born in 1922 in Man Peng Loi village, Lashio township, Shan State. Joined the Burma Frontier Force, Lashio Battalion. Led resistance against the Japanese in the Kachin Hills during World War II; Jamedar in the British-organized Northern Kachin Levies. Twice awarded the Burma Gallantry Medal by the British for his role in the anti-Japanese resistance. Captain in the 1st Kachin Rifles in 1946; fought against the CPB in the Irrawaddy Delta region in 1948. Defected to the Karen rebels along with his battalion in February 1949. Led "the Upper Burma campaign" against the Rangoon government and set up the Pawngyawng National Defense Force (PNDP), the first Kachin rebel army in Burma in November 1949. Retreated into China from Möng Ko in northeastern Shan State in April 1950. In exile along with a few hundred followers in China's Guizhou province until 1968. Vice military commander (under Than Shwe) of the first CPB unit that entered Burma on January 1, 1968. Military commander of the Northeastern Command in September 1969. Died under mysterious circumstances in the Wa Hills on March 9, 1972.

NOOM PAN, Sai

Shan. Born in 1940 in Möng Yang, eastern Shan State. Educated in Roman Catholic schools and at Rangoon University where he participated in the July 1962 demonstrations. Joined the Shan National Army (SNA) in Kengtung in 1967 and was hired by the CIA as a mercenary in Laos. Returned to Shan State and became a military commander under Khun Myint. Commander of the CPB's 768 Brigade when it was set up in August 1976, but never joined the party. His deputy was Sao Khun Sa (alias) Michael Davies, a Shan-Welsh rebel commander. Joined the April 1989 mutiny. Michael Davies was assassinated in May 1989. Unable to accept the accommodation with the military regime in Rangoon, Sai Noom Pan committed suicide in April 1990.

PE TINT, Thakin

Born in 1916 in Thaton. Grew up in Ye Ni between Pyinamana and Toungoo where in the 1930s he participated in the nationalist movement. Secretary in one of the ministries in Dr Ba Maw's puppet government during the Japanese occupation; later joined the anti-Japanese struggle and was sent to Bhamo in the Kachin Hills to contact Detachment 101 (the US-organized resistance in northern Burma). Party secretary in the Pyinmana area after World War II. Went underground in March 1948 and became member of the Central Committee in the same year. Peasant organizer in the Pyinmana area in the 1950s and later in the Pegu Yoma. Sent to China in 1965 to cement ties between exiles in Beijing and units at home. Went to Tirana in 1967 together with Khin Maung Gyi to attend the Fifth Congress of the Albanian Party of Labor. Elected vice chairman after the death of Thakin Zin and Thakin Chit in 1975. Stayed in China with Thakin Ba Thein Tin until 1978 when the CPB's central office moved to Panghsang headquarters. Left for China for medical treatment in 1986.

PHEUNG KYA-SHIN

Kokang Chinese. Officer in Jimmy Yang's Kokang Revolutionary Force in the 1960s; contacted by CPB cadres in China in July 1967 and promised arms and ammunition. Went to Beijing along with his younger brother Pheung Kya-fu shortly afterwards.

Michael Davies, alias Sao Khun Sa, Shan-Welsh rebel commander.
Photo: CPB Archives.

Sai Noom Pan. Photo: Hseng Noung Lintner.

Thakin Pe Tint, last vice-chairman of the CPB. Photo: CPB Archives.

Soe Thein, Political Commissar of the Northeastern Division.
Photo: Hseng Noung Lintner.

Entered Kokang from China on January 5, 1968 as commander of the Kokang People's Liberation Army, which officially merged with the CPB's army in August of same year. Led civil administration in Kokang although he never joined the party. Initiated the mutiny in March 1989 together with his younger brother.

SOE, Thakin

Born in 1905 in Moulmein. Employee of the Burmah Oil Company. Joined the Dohbama Asiayone and the CPB in the 1930s. Organized anti-Japanese guerrillas in Pyapon district, 1943–1945; split with the main CPB in August 1946, set up the Communist Party (Red Flag) and went underground in the Irrawaddy Delta region. Captured by the Burmese Army in November 1970 at his Than Chaung camp near the Arakan Yoma. Imprisoned but released during the 1980 amnesty. In retirement until he re-entered politics in August 1988. Patron of the Unity and Development Party in September; died in Rangoon on May 4, 1989.

SOE THEIN

Born in 1925 in Sagaing. Joined the Burma Independence Army (BIA) in 1942 and the CPB in 1943. Fought against the Japanese in upper Burma together with his cousin Kyin Maung. Both went underground with the CPB in March 1948. CPB brigade commander in the Meiktila-Mandalay-Kyaukse area in 1950. Vice secretary of the Kyaukse District party committee. Went to the Pegu Yoma in April 1950 and to China in 1951. Stayed in Sichuan until 1968, when the northeastern base area was set up. Political commissar of the first CPB until that entered the northeast in 1968. Vice political commissar of the Northeastern Command in September 1969. Member of the Central Committee in 1975. Political commissar of the Northeastern Region in 1985. Arrested by the mutineers in the Wa Hills in April 1989.

TAIK AUNG

Born in Waw, Pegu District, of a peasant family. Educated in a Buddhist village monastery. Joined the CPB in the 1940s; went to China in 1953. Stayed in Sichuan, 1953–1963. One of the Beijing Returnees. Led the bloody purges in the Pegu Yoma in the 1960s. Went to the Northeastern Base Area in 1969; member of the Central Committee in 1975. Commander of the Panghsang security force and second in command of the Northeastern Command; considered a hardliner. Went to the Central Bureau along with Khin Maung Gyi and Mya Min in 1980; returned to Panghsang after suffering a stroke in 1983. Went to China to get medical treatment in the same year.

THAN MYAING, Thakin

Active in the Dohbama Asiayone. In charge of radio propaganda for Dr Ba Maw's puppet government during the Japanese occupation. Became member of the CPB's Central Committee at the Second Congress in 1945 and member of the Politbureau in 1953. Went to China in 1953; stayed in Sichuan province. Member of the "leading group of five" in China in November 1963; purged for "revisionism" in 1967. Interned in a Chinese prison camp until 1973 when he was released. Settled in Sichuan where he still lives.

THAN SHWE

Joined the Burma Independence Army (BIA) in 1942 and attended the Officers' Training School in Rangoon during the Japanese occupation. Went to China with *yebaw* Aung Gyi in 1950. In Sichuan, China 1950–1968. Member of the "leading group of five" in China in November 1963. Military commander of the first CPB unit that entered Burma from China on January 1, 1968. Political commissar of the Northeastern Command in September 1969. Member of the Central Committee in 1975; demoted to ordinary party member in 1980 for advocating a peaceful settlement with the government. Left the party in 1985 and retired in China.

THAN TUN, Thakin

Born in 1911 in Pyinmana. School teacher and member of the Dohbama Asiayone. Joined the CPB shortly after its foundation in August 1939. Active in the anti-Japanese resistance during World War II. Aung San's brother-in-law. General secretary of the Anti-Fascist People's Freedom League (AFPFL) from May 1946 until the CPB was expelled from the front in August. Went to Calcutta in February 1948 to attended the Second Congress of the Communist Party of India. *De facto* leader of the CPB after the Second Congress in 1945. Took the CPB underground in March 1948. Elected first party chairman in 1950 (prior to this, the party had been headed by a general secretary) and retained that post until he was killed in the Pegu Yoma on September 24, 1968.

THEIN PE, Thakin (alias) Thein Pe Myint

Born in 1914 in Budalin, Lower Chindwin District. Attended Mandalay Intermediate College and graduated from Rangoon University in 1934. One of the leaders of the 1936 student strike in Rangoon; active in the Dohbama Asiayone. Studied law at Calcutta University; closely associated with revolutionary organizations in Bengal. Member of the CPB in 1939, but not one of its founders. Went to India during World War II to obtain Allied assistance in the struggle against the Japanese. Elected general secretary of the CPB in absentia at the Second Congress in 1945. Returned to Burma shortly afterwards and became editor of the party's theoretical organ *People's Power* or *Pyithu Ana* (ပြည်သူ့ အာဏာ). Left the CPB on March 26, 1948, two days before it went underground and resorted to armed struggle. One of Burma's leading writers in the 1950s and 1960s. Elected to parliament for Budalin on a National Unity Front ticket in 1956. Editor of the leftist *Vanguard* newspaper. Became adviser to General Ne Win's military government after the 1962 coup d'etat and joined the ruling Burma Socialist Program Party (BSPP). Died in Rangoon in 1978. Considered Burma's first Communist.

TIN MYA, Thakin

Born in Danubyu. Member of the Dohbama Asiayone. Political commissar of the No 7 Military Region of the Burma National Army (BNA) in 1945. Became an alternate member of the CPB's Central Committee in 1945. Joined Thakin Soe's Red Flag faction in March 1946 but was expelled in 1949 and rejoined the CPB. Arrested in 1957; released in 1960. Briefly rearrested in 1962. Joined the ruling Burma Socialist Program Party (BSPP) and became a member of its Central Committee. Author of a five-volume work on the anti-Japanese struggle during World War II. Expressed support for the 1988 pro-democracy movement in Rangoon but took no active part in it. Lives in retirement in Rangoon.

TIN YEE (alias) Ne Win

Born in 1922 in Waw, Pegu District. Participated in the "1300 Movement" and the Dohbama Asiayone in Pegu. Joined the CPB during the anti-Japanese struggle in 1943. Went to China in 1951 and stayed in Sichuan until 1968. Member of the "leading group of five" in China in November 1963. Political commissar of the 404 War Zone (the Kokang forces), 1968–1969; he was then known as "Yang Koang." Political commissar of the Northeastern Command in 1971. Member of the Central Commitee and the Politbureau in 1975. Chief of General Staff of the CPB's army from 1986 until the mutiny. Fled to China in April 1989.

YAN AUNG, Bo (alias) Thakin Hla Myaing.

Born in 1908 in Syriam. Active in the Dohbama Asiayone; organized the oil workers in Syriam. Member of the Marxist study group in 1939. Went with Aung San to Amoy, China, and on to Japan in 1940. One of the Thirty Comrades. Arrested when the CPB went underground on March 28, 1948, but was freed shortly afterwards to negotiate with the party. Remained with the CPB, but was considered almost a "traitor." He was nevertheless elected to the Central Committee and stayed in the Pegu Yoma until he was executed there on December 26, 1967.

YE HTUT, Bo (alias) Thakin Aung Thein

Born in 1922 in Rangoon. Member of the Dohbama Asiayone; one of the Thirty Comrades. Commanding officer in the Burmese Army after independence. One of the mutineers from the 3rd Burifs (Burma Rifles) who went underground in 1949. Vice chief of General Staff when the Revolutionary Burma Army (RBA) joined the CPB's People's Liberation Army of Burma in 1950 to become the People's Army. Surrendered in June 1963. Later joined the ruling Burma Socialist Program Party (BSPP) and became member of its Central Committee. Quit the BSPP and participated in the 1988 pro-democracy uprising in Burma.

ZAU MAI

Kachin. Born in 1932 in Kutkai, northeastern Shan State. Joined Naw Seng's forces in 1949. Stayed with him in China, 1950–1968. Entered Möng Ko on January 1, 1968 together with Naw Seng's troops and the CPB's political commissars. Vice military commander of the Northeastern Command in September 1969. Succeeded Naw Seng as commander after the latter's death in 1972. Member of the Central Committee in 1975. Joined the 1989 mutiny and became one of the leaders of the new Burma National United Party (BNUP), now renamed the United Wa State Party (UWSP).

ZEYA, Bo (alias) Thakin Hla Maung

Born in 1920. Educated at Rangoon University and president of the Students' Union, 1940–1941. One of the Thirty Comrades. Chief of General Staff of the Burma Defense Army (BDA), 1942–1943. Commander of the 3rd Burifs (Burma Rifles) after the war. Joined the army mutiny in 1949 and set up the Revolutionary Burma Army (RBA) and became second vice chairman of the "Central People's Revolutionary Military Commission" when the RBA and the People's Liberation Army of Burma merged to become the People's Army on September 1, 1950. Went to China in 1953; one of the Beijing Returnees who participated in the 1963 peace talks. Killed in action near the Pegu Yoma on April 16, 1968.

ZHANG ZHI MING (alias) Kyi Myint

Chinese. Born in 1950 in Wanting, China's Yunnan province. Joined the CPB in 1968 as a volunteer along with Li Ziru and Lin Ming Xian. One of the CPB's ablest military officers. Commander of the 2nd Brigade at Möng Paw; led the assault on Hsi-Hsinwan in November 1986. Supported the mutiny in April 1989 and joined Lin Ming Xian's forces in the former 815 Region (Mekong River Division) in eastern Shan State in May.

ZIN, Thakin

Born in 1912 in Daik-U. Timber merchant. Active in the Dohbama Asiayone. Joined the CPB in 1943. Became a member of the Central Commitee at the Second Congress in 1945. Organizer in the All-Burma Peasants' Organization (ABPO). Went underground in March 1948. Political commissar of the CPB's Southern Burma Command in the 1950s. Party chairman after the death of Thakin Than Tun in October 1968. Killed in the Pegu Yoma on March 15, 1975.

The new Central Committee at the Third Party Congress, Panghsang, September–October 1985. Front row, left to right: Pe Htaung, Ye Tun, Tin Yee, Khin Maung Gyi, Thakin Ba Thein Tin, Myo Myint, Kyaw Mya, Kyin Maung, Mya Min. Back row, left to right: Aye Ngwe, Kyaw Myint, Li Ziru, Tint Hlaing, Chao Ngi Lai, Kyaw Zaw, Sai Aung Win, San Thu, Tun Lwin, unknown, Zau Mai, Soe Thein. Photo: CPB Archives.

Appendix I
Organization of the CPB
Prior to the 1989 Mutiny

The CPB's Third Congress, held at Panghsang from September 9 to October 2, 1985, elected a new 29-member Central Committee comprising the following personalities:

Politbureau:

Thakin Ba Thein Tin, Chairman	*Sichuan lao ping.*
Thakin Pe Tint, Vice Chairman	"Old Comrade" from Pyinmana who joined the *Sichuan lao pings* in China in 1965.
Khin Maung Gyi, secretary to the CC.	*Sichuan lao ping.*
Myo Myint a.k.a. U Aung	"Old Comrade" from the Pegu Yoma.
Kyaw Mya	"Old Comrade" from Arakan.
Kyin Maung a.k.a. *yebaw* Tun	"Old Comrade" from the Kyawkku base area.
Tin Yee a.k.a. Ne Win	*Sichuan lao ping.* Chief of Staff of the CPB's People's Army.

Other CC Members:

Kyaw Zaw	"Newcomer"; joined the CPB in 1976.
Saw Han	"Old Comrade" from Tavoy.
San Thu	*Sichuan lao ping.*
Soe Thein	*Sichuan lao ping.*
Soe Lwin	"Old Comrade" from Tavoy.
Sai Aung Win	Shan. Joined the CPB in Henzada in 1964.
Zau Mai	*Guizhou lao ping.*
Tun Lwin a.k.a. Ye Din	*Sichuan lao ping.*
Hpalang Gam Di	*Guizhou lao ping.*
Pe Htaung a.k.a. Ba Tan	*Sichuan lao ping.*
Mya Min	"Old Comrade" from Pyinmana.
Ye Tun	"Old Comrade" from Pyinmana.
Aye Ngwe	*Sichuan lao ping.*
Aye Hla	"Old Comrade" from Tavoy.

Alternate members of the CC:

Kyaw Myint	*Sichuan lao ping.*
Chao Ngi Lai	Wa. Joined the CPB in 1968.

Saw Ba Moe	Karen. Joined the CPB in 1973.
Tint Hlaing	*Sichuan lao ping.*
Tun Tin	Karen. *Guizhou lao ping.*
Pao Yo Chang	Wa. Joined the CPB in 1968.
Mya Thaung	*Sichuan lao ping.*
Li Ziru	Chinese volunteer. Joined the CPB in 1968.

1) *Sichuan lao pings*	9 members + 3 alternates
2) "Old Comrades"	8 members + 0 alternates
3) *Guizhou lao pings*	2 members + 1 alternates
4) Newcomers	1 members + 0 alternates
5) Chinese volunteers	0 members + 1 alternates
6) Minority cadres	1 members + 3 alternates

Zau Mai, Sai Aung Win, Pao Yo Chang, Chao Ngi Lai, Tun Tin, Saw Ba Moe, and Li Ziru joined the mutineers. Hpalang Gam Di retired in China shortly after the Third Congress. All the Burman leaders (except the three who are based in Tavoy, Tenasserim) fled to China in April 1989. Soe Thein and Mya Thaung were arrested by mutineers in the northern Wa Hills.

"The People's Army"—Organization.

A 6-member Central Military Commission served as the CPB's "high command" until the 1989 mutiny:

Thakin Ba Thein Tin, Chairman.
Tin Yee, Chief of Staff of the People's Army.
Kyaw Zaw, Vice Chief of Staff of the People's Army.
Zau Mai, commander, Northeastern Command (NEC).
Pe Tint
Myo Myint

There were three different types of armed personnel:
1) Regular Army	approx. 10,000 men;
2) District and township forces	approx. 5,000 men;
3) Local militia units	(unspecified).

The regular army consisted of 11 brigades plus 7 independent battalions:

Northern Bureau forces:

1st Brigade	Mogok, Möng Mit;
2nd Brigade	Möng Ko (formerly the 303 War Zone);
3rd Brigade	Shweli river valley (formerly the 202 War Zone).

+ local district forces in Northern Kachin State District (formerly the 101 War Zone).
Total: 1,500 men.

Northeastern Region:

6th Brigade	headquartered at Wan Ho-tao, Northern Kengtung District but operated mainly around Möng Hsat near the Thai border;

7th Brigade   headquartered at Manghseng, Southern Wa District;
12th Brigade   headquartered at Möng Mau, Northern Wa District;
768 Brigade   the Möng Yang area, Northern Kengtung District;
851 Brigade   central security at Panghsang;
859 Brigade   Northern Kengtung District.
Total: 6,000–7,000 men.

Mekong River Division:

9th Brigade   headquartered at Keng Khan;
11th Brigade   headquartered at Möng La;
The 1st and 3rd Battalions operated in the guerrilla zone immediately south of the Nam Loi river; the 14th Battalion operated in the mountain range northwest of Möng Pa Liao.
Total: 1,200–1,300 men.

Central Bureau forces:

4045 Battalion   Möng Nai;
4046 Battalion   Lankhö/Wan Hat;
4047 Battalion   Loi Tsang;
502 Battalion   Lai Hka.
+ *the Shan State Nationalities Liberation Organization* (SSNLO), a Pa-O domi-nated rebel army which operates in the hills southeast of Taunggyi and is led by Tha Kalei;
the Kayan New Land Council (KNLC) in the hills west of Pekon and Möng Pai, led by Shwe Aye a.k.a. Naing Lu Hta;
and *the Karenni Nationalities Liberation Front* or the *ka la la ta* , a CPB-affiliated Karenni (Kayah) rebel army (ကလလတ ; ကရင်နီ လူမျိုး ပေါင်းစုံ လွတ်မြောက်ရေး တပ်ဦး:)
Total: 1,700–1,800 men.

Other areas:

Tenasserim Division, 100–200 men, and Arakan State, 50–100 men. By November 1989, these two groups were the only armed CPB units left in Burma.

The monument in Möng Ko commemorating the CPB push into northeastern Burma on January 1, 1968. Photo: Bertil Lintner.

APPENDIX II
THE CPB'S BASE AREAS AND GUERRILLA ZONES PRIOR TO THE 1989 MUTINY

Before fierce fighting broke out between the CPB and government forces in November 1986, the CPB controlled and administered a 20,000 square kilometer area along the Chinese frontier in northeastern Shan and Kachin states with a total population of 460,000 people. For administrative and military purposes, this area was divided into the Northern Bureau, the Northeastern Region, and the Mekong River Division. In January 1987 the CPB lost about 500 square kilometers of this territory, but retained control over all other areas until the 1989 mutiny.

This territory, with its own administration, infrastructure, schools, and hospitals, formed a *de facto* buffer state between Burma and China A string of heavily fortified camps defended the "border" between the CPB area and the government-controlled territory to the west of it; usually, a CPB camp would be located just opposite a Burmese Army camp in an "eyeball-to-eyeball" standoff. Inside this firmly controlled base area, CPB army presence would be limited to local forces and lightly armed militiamen whose main duty was to maintain law and order.

In western Shan State a number of loosely defined guerrilla zones made up the CPB's Central Bureau. In addition, smaller groups of CPB guerrillas operated in Kayah State, Tenasserim Division, and along the Bangladesh border in Arakan State.

NORTHERN BUREAU AREAS

Prior to the government offensive against the CPB in early 1987 and the 1989 mutiny, four base areas and one guerrilla zone were under the supervision of the CPB's Northern Bureau, headquartered at Möng Ko:
1) Northern Kachin State District (base area);
2) Northern Shan State District (guerrilla zone);
3) Namkham District (base area);
4) Panghsai Special Township (base area);
5) Kutkai District (base area).

The four base areas totalled 4,000 square kilometers with a population of 57,000 people; the guerrilla zone was a loosely defined area south of the Shweli river. In all these areas, there were about 1,500–2,000 CPB regulars plus about 500 soldiers

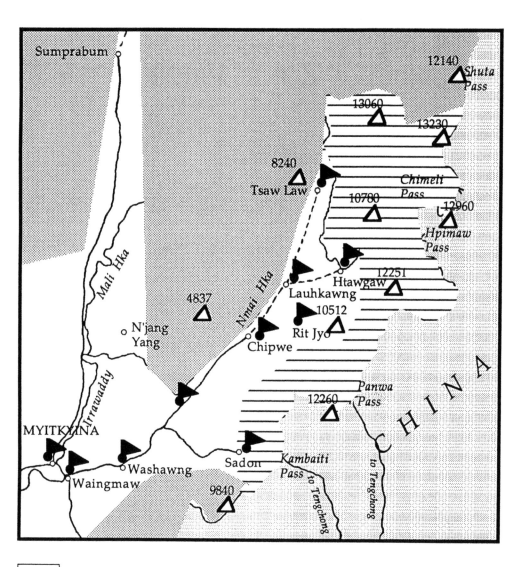

Map 1. Northern Kachin State District (formerly 101 War Zone)

organized in various local forces and an unspecified number of village militiamen. Two Politbureau members—Myo Myint a.k.a. U Aung and Kyin Maung a.k.a. *yebaw* Tun—and three other members of the Central Committee—Sai Aung Win (full CC member), Pe Htaung a.k.a. Ba Tan (full CC member), and Tun Tin (alternate member of the CC)—were based at Möng Ko before the mutiny.

NORTHERN KACHIN STATE DISTRICT

Area: Approx. 2,000 square kilometers. in eastern Kachin State, from the headquarters at Kambaiti Pass in the south to Chimeli Pass and the Hkyawng No Hka river in the north. Headquarters at Kambaiti Pass near the Chinese border.

Population: This is a sparsely populated, mountainous region with less than 1,000 inhabitants. All of these belong to various Kachin tribes, mainly Atzis, Lashis, and Marus with a sprinkling of Lisus and a smaller tribe, the Ngoshans.

Economy and infrastructure: "Slash-and-burn" shifting cultivation of hill paddy, plus some poppy cultivation around Kambaiti in the south. The Kachin Independence Army (KIA) supplies the cadres and troops with rations in exchange for arms and ammunition. Opium is sold to merchants from Myitkyina, Mogaung, and other government-controlled towns in Kachin State. Timber export to China provides additional income. There are no roads in the area, only mule tracks. A small clinic is maintained at Hpimaw.

Representation in the 1985 Central Committee: None. All the leaders are Kachins, the troops mostly Kachins except for one company of Wa soldiers who were sent up to the area in 1985. Previously a Burman political commissar, Toe Shein, was based at Kambaiti, but he was withdrawn to Panghsang in 1985 and replaced by Sumlut Naw, a *Guizhou lao ping*.

Troop strength: Only a few hundred, but they are well armed with mortars, medium machine-guns, and anti-aircraft guns. Military operations are usually carried out in close cooperation with the KIA. There is a string of Burmese Army camps opposite the former CPB camps along the Chinese frontier in Kachin State: at Tsawlaw, Lauhkawng, Htawgaw, Chipwe, Rit Jyo, and Sadon.

History: This area was founded by two former local commanders of the KIA, Ting Ying and Zalum, who defected to the CPB with 400 men in 1968. They received massive support from the Chinese and their territory became the 101 War Zone, one of several base areas the CPB set up along the northeastern frontier in the late 1960s. Fierce fighting broke out with the KIA, which lasted until a ceasefire agreement was reached between the Kachin rebels and the CPB in 1976. Following the truce, cooperation between the two rebel armies became close: representatives from the 101 War Zone told this writer in March 1986 (well before the mutiny) that "there are no longer any political differences between us and the KIA."

The situation in 1990: Ting Ying and Zalum are still the leaders of this area and they maintain some contact with other CPB mutineers in Shan State. Although attempts were made by the main group of mutineers at Panghsang to form a united front with other former CPB forces based along the Chinese frontier, Ting Ying and

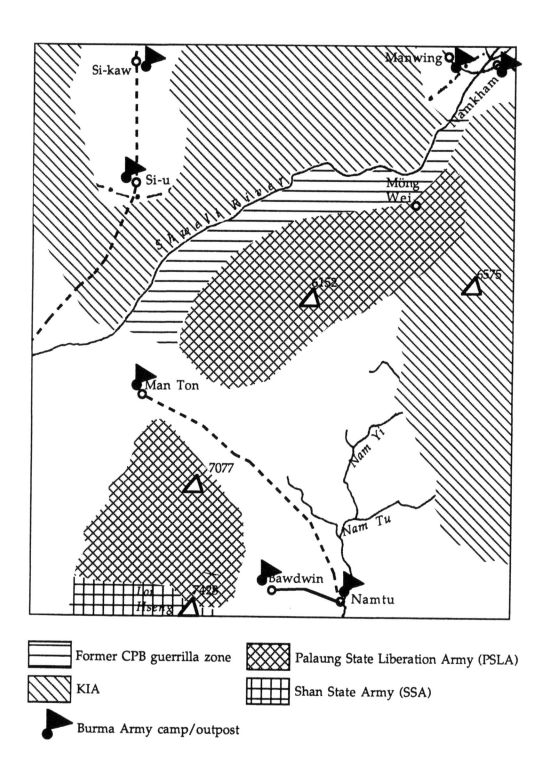

Former CPB guerrilla zone

KIA

Burma Army camp/outpost

Palaung State Liberation Army (PSLA)

Shan State Army (SSA)

Map 2. Northern Shan State District (formerly 202 War Zone)

Zalum set up their own People's Liberation Front (PLF; ပြည်သူ့ လွတ်မြောက်ရေး တပ်ဦး) in 1989 and in effect joined forces with the KIA.

NORTHERN SHAN STATE DISTRICT

Area: 500–600 square kilometers on the southern bank of the Shweli river, from Man Ton, north of Namtu, up to the hills immediately west of Namkham. The main village in the area, Möng Wei, was contested by the CPB and the government forces. The area is sandwiched between the KIA-controlled territory north of the Shweli and the areas of operation of the Shan State Army (SSA) and the Palaung State Liberation Army (PSLA) to the south.

Population: Mostly Shan and Palaung.

Economy and infrastructure: The 12 villages in "Möng Wei guerrilla township" are relatively poor, being dependent on wet paddy cultivation (the Shan villages) or hill paddy and tea (the Palaung villages). There are no roads in the area.

Representation in the 1985 Central Committee: None. No political commissars from the CPB were permanently based in this area.

Troop strength: This was formerly the area of operation of the CPB's 3rd Brigade and it was known as "the 202 War Zone," or "the Military Expansion Area." It was meant to be the bridgehead from which the northeastern forces would reach Burma proper north of Mandalay—a scheme which never materialized since the Burmese Army camp at Man Ton prevented any such expansion westwards along the Shweli river. Previously the 3rd Brigade comprised more than 1,000 men; today, its strength is estimated at 300— most of them are based at Möng Ko, not in this guerrilla zone.

History: The Shweli river valley—and the hills surrounding the garrison town of Möng Mit and the ruby mines at Mogok—are old CPB strongholds, dating back to the 1950s. It was not, however, until 1968 that the forces here were properly armed with new Chinese weapons, and serious attempts were made to reach the plains north of Mandalay. In order to facilitate this plan, "the 202 War Zone" linked up with SSA troops in the hills surrounding Möng Mit; the town itself was briefly captured by Communist troops in April 1977. But clashes also erupted with Shan as well as Palaung rebels over the question of which army should collect taxes from the local villages. The last such clash occurred in August 1986, forcing most CPB troops to leave the area. The SSA and the PSLA have always enjoyed more popular support than the CPB in this region.

The situation in 1990: There were still a few ex-CPB troops along the Shweli river in 1990, but they maintained no permanent camps. The former 3rd Brigade was controlled by the Kokang-led mutineers at Möng Ko.

NAMKHAM DISTRICT

Area: Two enclaves of Burmese territory opposite the town of Namkham, north of the Shweli river—Khun Hai and Man Hio—totalling 124 square kilometers.

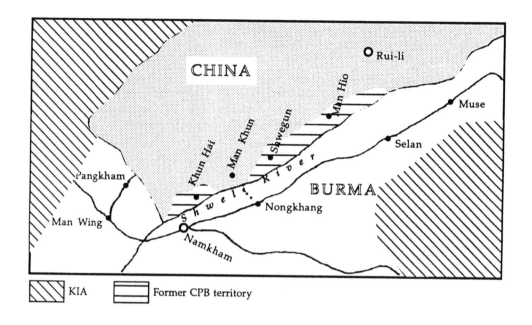

Map 3. Namkham District (recaptured by the Burmese Army on January 13, 1987).

Population: 9,211 (1986). The vast majority are Shans, plus a few Kachins and Chinese. Under CPB administration the area consisted of five village tracts.

Economy and Infrastructure: Namkham used to be the richest agricultural district in the CPB's northeastern base area since it produced a surplus of paddy, sugar cane, pulses, soya beans, fruit, and vegetables. Khun Hai is the home of the famous Namkham tobacco, which was—and still is—sold to other parts of Burma as well as across the border to China.

Representation in the 1985 Central Committee: None. The area was administered from the Northern Bureau headquarters at Möng Ko.

Troop strength: There were only a few hundred local township forces and militiamen, no regular CPB troops.

History: The CPB first infiltrated the Khun Hai and Man Hio enclaves in February 1968 by establishing links with two local SSA commanders in the area, Saya Mong and Bo Kang Yoi. The last government troops were withdrawn to Namkham, Selan, and other towns south of the Shweli river in August 1968. The CPB remained in control of the area until heavy fighting broke out between government forces and Communist troops in northeastern Shan State in November 1986. On January 13, 1987 the Burmese Army crossed the Shweli river and recaptured both Khun Hai and Man Hio. Some reports indicate that the government forces also passed through Chinese territory to retake these two enclaves.

The situation in 1990: Since the loss of Khun Hai and Man Hio two years ago, the CPB has been unable to re-infiltrate the area. Today it is firmly controlled by the Burmese government and has become a major center for the now legal border trade between China and Burma.

PANGHSAI SPECIAL TOWNSHIP AND KUTKAI DISTRICT

Area: 2,164 square kilometers (1986); now approx. 1,800 square kilometers. In January 1987 the Burmese government regained control over Panghsai (Kyu-hkok), the nearby market town of Möng Paw, and some surrounding areas. Möng Paw had previously constituted one township in the CPB's administration; the Communists retained control over the other four rebel townships in the CPB's Kutkai District: Yawng Ni (center: Möng Ko headquarters), Möng Hom (including Möng Ya), Möng Si, and Nam Kyaun.

Population: 47,060 (1986), of whom 6,000 lived in Panghsai Special Township (which had district status under the CPB administration) and 1,000 in Möng Paw. About 40,000 people—Kachins, Chinese, Shans, Palaungs, Lisu, Miao (Hmong), and Hkala—still live in insurgent-controlled areas.

Economy and Infrastructure: Panghsai used to be the main transfer point for Chinese consumer goods entering Burma unofficially. Tax levied by the CPB on cross-border trade with China became increasingly important in the late 1970s, when Beijing severely cut back its aid to the Burmese Communists and told the party that it had to become self-reliant. During this period, the tax amounted to Kyats 27 million annually, or nearly 50 percent of the party's then Kyats 56 million annual budget. Originally only the CPB was allowed by the Chinese to act as a middle-man in this trade. The revenue declined, however, in 1980, when China decided to discontinue the CPB's monopoly on the cross-border trade. From then on traders also began to do business with China through the government-controlled corridor near Namkham. Although the Burmese government did not regain much territory in January 1987, when Panghsai and Möng Paw were recaptured, the effects on the CPB's economy were substantial. In 1988, Panghsai was opened for legal border trade between China and Burma, and money that formerly went to the CPB's coffers was redirected to Rangoon.

The valleys of Möng Paw, Möng Ko, Möng Hom, and Möng Ya have a large Shan population who grow wet paddy, fruit, and vegetables. The Chinese and the tribal people in the hills surrounding the valleys grow opium. The Burmese government claimed shortly after the recapture of Panghsai that they had found a heroin refinery in the town, but this seems to be mere propaganda. It is unlikely that the CPB could have maintained such an operation so close to the Chinese border. Contrary to official claims that the operation against this area in early 1987 was part of an "anti-narcotics drive," there is no indication that the people in the areas recaptured by government forces have switched to other crops. Nor has the region's lucrative opium trade been affected in any way.

The CPB built a hydroelectric power station near Möng Ko with Chinese help in the late 1960s, but it has been in operation only sporadically. Until the 1986/87 offensive, trucks, jeeps, and tractors plied the dirt roads which connect Panghsai, Möng Paw, and Möng Ko; since then, the CPB has controlled only the last 15 kms.

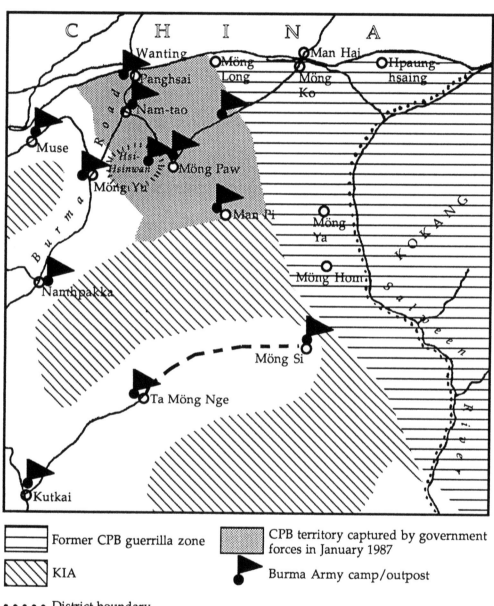

Former CPB guerrilla zone

CPB territory captured by government forces in January 1987

KIA

Burma Army camp/outpost

• • • • • District boundary

Map 4. Kutkai District

stretch of the Möng Paw-Möng Ko road. There is a primary school at Möng Ko and a relatively well-equipped hospital.

Representation in the 1985 Central Committee: See above.

Troop Strength: Prior to the 1989 mutiny, the CPB maintained three brigades in this area: the 1st, the 2nd, and the 3rd, plus a special force and an artillery unit, apart from local militia. These units formed the core of the mutiny in March 1989 and their present strength is as follows:

1st Brigade (Mogok, Möng Mit) 200–300 men
2nd Brigade (Möng Ko)   750 men: 500 regulars plus 150 special force and 100 artillery.
3rd Brigade (the Shweli river) 300 men.

Most of the troops are Wa, Kachin, Shan, Palaung, and ethnic Chinese.

History: Kutkai District was the first "liberated area" along the Chinese border. Möng Ko was taken over when the CPB made its push across the frontier on January 1, 1968. A year later, the CPB expanded its territory to Möng Hom, Möng Ya, and the hills around Möng Si. On March 21, 1970, Möng Paw was taken over by the CPB. Panghsai was captured on March 27, after a heavy, two-day battle. The Northern Bureau was set up at Möng Ko in December 1979. No territorial changes occurred until the government recaptured Panghsai, Möng Paw, Khun Hai, and Man Hio (approximately 500 square kilometers) in January 1987.

The situation in 1990: The Burmese government remains in firm control of the areas recaptured in January 1987, but has not managed to expand beyond them. On March 14, 1989, the Möng Ko forces (1st, 2nd, and 3rd Brigades, plus the local forces in Kokang District, were renamed the Burma National Democratic Alliance Army (မြန်မာပြည် အမျိုးသား ဒီမိုကရေစီ မဟာမိတ် တပ်မတော်), led by Pheung Kya-shin.

NORTHEASTERN REGION

The CPB's Northeastern Region, previously known as the Northeastern War Zone, comprised some of the most important base areas along the Chinese frontier: Kokang District, Northern Wa District, Southern Wa District, Northern Kengtung District, and a "special township" around the party headquarters at Panghsang. Together, these areas make up 14,200 square kilometers with 360,000 inhabitants.

KOKANG DISTRICT

Area: The total area of Kokang is 2,200 square kilometers of which 2,000 square kilometers are under rebel administration. The area is bordered by the Chinese frontier in the east and north, the Salween river in the west, and the Nam Ting river in the south. The CPB divided Kokang District into four townships: Hongshin, Chingwan, Yawng Hong, and Tongshan. The Burmese government's presence in Kokang was limited to the southern part near the towns of Kunlong and Hopang. The former CPB district headquarters was located at the eastern edge of the Malipa valley, near the Chinese border. This valley is the only plain in Kokang; the area is extremely mountainous. The narrow Chinsweho corridor connects Kokang with the insurgent territories to the south (Northern Wa District).

Map 5. Kokang District

Population: 70,239 (1986): 50,000 ethnic Chinese, 10,000 Palaungs (mostly in Ching-wan and Tongshan townships), and 10,000 Lisus (in Hongshin), Shans (the Malipa Valley), Miao or Hmong (Yawng Hong, Chingwan, and Hongshin), and Wa (Yawng Hong, Chingwan and Hongshin). Major towns in the area are Nangkaw in Yawng Hong township (300 houses), Lao Khai in the Malipa valley (200 houses), and Tashwehtang (100 houses).

Economy and Infrastructure: The area is poor and backward by any standards. Few households can grow paddy and Kokang traditionally has a yearly cycle of culti-vating opium poppies during the dry season and corn when the rains begin in May or June. Between these two crops, when the opium has been harvested but not yet sold and the corn is still too young to eat, most farmers in the hills face a month or so of near-starvation. Kokang tea was quite famous in the past, but production has declined considerably since the war broke out. Tea had to be carried to government-controlled market towns to be sold and the cash brought back along dangerous moun-tain trails, but this became unfeasible when the hills were turned into battle zones. Consequently, opium became the only viable cash crop. The Malipa valley is the only relatively rich farming area in Kokang, and the rice farmers there are consid-erably more affluent than the poppy growers in the hills. Because of these hard-ships, many Kokang Chinese have gone elsewhere in Burma and even to Thailand to look for employment and business opportunities.

A CPB-built motor road, along which Chinese consumer goods enter Burma, con-nects Lao Khai, Ching Khai and other villages in the Malipa valley with the Chinese border. Mule tracks connect all major villages in Kokang. There is a middle school in Lao Khai and 35 primary schools in major villages throughout Kokang. The medium of instruction is Chinese; very few Kokang Chinese speak Burmese. There is one small hospital at district headquarters and four clinics, one in each township, as well as two private clinics in Lao Khai. Lao Khai, Tashwehtang, and Nangkaw have generator-powered electricity.

Representation in the 1985 Central Committee: None. No Burman CPB political commissars were stationed in Kokang—only one ethnic Chinese CPB cadre from Tavoy.

Troop strength: Since Kokang is located well east of the CPB defense lines west of the Salween river (along the western borders of Kutkai District), there were no regular CPB troops in Kokang, only local township forces and militia, totaling about 500–700 men. These are still positioned mainly along the "frontline" in the Chinsweho corridor, opposite the government outposts in the southern part of the district.

History: During the British time, colonial rule hardly extended east of the Sal-ween. It could, at best, be described as indirect rule through the British advised *sawbwa* , or prince, of Hsenwi, west of the river, to whom the lesser *sawbwa* of Kokang, east of the river, paid tribute. Independent Burma's rulers were even less successful than the British in bringing Kokang under control. In the early 1950s, the area was invaded by retreating Kuomintang forces from China who forged alliances with local warlords. One of them, Lo Hsing-han, later joined the government as a home guard commander and was allowed to traffic in drugs in exchange for fighting the insurgents. When the CPB was planning its push into the northeast in the late 1960s, it contacted a rival warlord, Pheung Kya-shin, and Kokang was penetrated with his assistance. The CPB entered Kokang from the Chinese side on January 5, 1968, and by the end of the year had taken over most of the area. A "People's Government of Kokang" was set up on September 8, 1969 to formalize the CPB's rule. The westward expansion of the CPB was halted in 1971 during the crucial 45-day battle for Kunlong bridge, which connects Kokang with the area west of the Salween. After that the situation remained static until the 1989 mutiny.

The situation in 1990: On March 12, 1989, Kokang became the first area to rebel against the old CPB leadership, as well as the first break-away faction to contact the Rangoon authorities. Brig-Gen Khin Nyunt from the State Law and Order Restoration Council (SLORC) in Rangoon visited Chinsweho on August 25 and provided 2,000 bags of rice as well as 5 million Kyats in "development aid." Kokang chieftain Pheung Kya-shin heads the Burma National Democratic Alliance Army (မန်မာပြည် အမျိုးသား ဒီမိုကရေစီ မဟာမိတ် တပ်မတော်).

NORTHERN WA DISTRICT

Area: The northern Wa Hills (bordered by the Chinese frontier in the east, the Salween in the west, the Namting river in the north, and the Nam Nang river in the south) cover 6,124 square kilometers of which the insurgents control 5,824 square kilometers. The government controls the 300 square kilometer area around Hopang and Panglong and the motor road between these two towns. The government-controlled area is lowland; the rest consists of steep mountain ranges and deep river gorges, with the sole exception of the plain near the Namting river and the Shan-inhabited Na Hpan valley. For administrative purposes, the CPB divided the district into 12 townships: Ywinching, Kyinshan, Na Wi, Kungming Shan, Saohpa, Khun Ma, Wanling, Man Tong, Ai Kyin, Yinfang (Vingngun), Linghaw, and Kalung Pa. District headquarters is located at Möng Mau in Kungming Shan.

Population: 171,176 lived in the insurgent-controlled Northern Wa Hills in 1986: 90 percent Wa and 10 percent others, mainly Chinese, Shan (Na Hpan in Yinfang), Lahu, and Kachin (Na Wi). This should be compared with 184,621 in 1979. Many families moved out of the insurgent-controlled area to escape having their sons drafted into the CPB army. The 1986 population figure also reflects the outcome of the CPB's costly human waves tactics: 78,944 were males compared to 92,232 females. Many Wa in the northern part of the district are Baptist Christians, converted by American missionaries in the 1950s. In the south around Vingngun, Shan-Buddhist influence is evident. In between lies the "Wild Wa" heartland around the villages of Khun Ma and Ai Kyin, where the local people were headhunters until the arrival of the CPB in the early 1970s.

Economy and Infrastructure: The area is extremely poor; rats often destroy vegetables, corn, hill paddy, and other edible crops. Wet paddy is cultivated only in Na Hpan. Most of the area is too mountainous even for hill paddy, and opium (which rats cannot eat—an important consideration for the local people) remains the main cash crop. A notable exception is the northern part around Möng Mau and Saohin-Saohpa near the Chinese border, where the missionaries introduced oranges a few decades ago. Oranges are exported to China and provide the cultiva

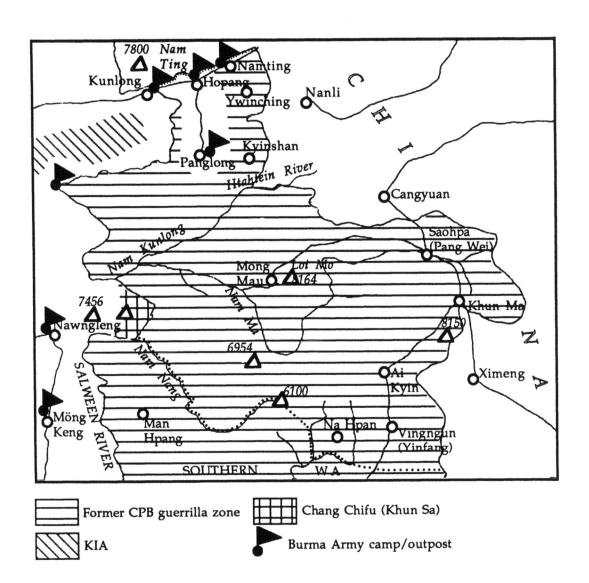

Map 6. Northern Wa District

tors with cash with which to buy rice. The Namting river valley is a major trade route from China to Kunlong and on to Lashio and northern Burma. The rebels collect tax on this trade.

Before the CPB took over the area in the early 1970s, the motor road to Panglong continued up to Möng Mau. That road was destroyed shortly after the CPB's takeover. In its place, the CPB began an ambitious road-building project to connect Möng Mau with Saohpa on the Chinese frontier, and from there over the hills down to Panghsang. For many years, only the stretch to Saohpa (and across the frontier to Cangyuan in China) was completed and usable for motor traffic (lorries, tractors, and motorcycles); the entire road was finally inaugurated in 1988. There is also a CPB-built motor road from Khun Ma to Ximeng in China. The old road from Kunlong to Hopang along the Namting to China is cut just east of Hopang, but is still used by traders.

The CPB maintained a badly equipped hospital at Möng Mau. There is no electricity in the entire district. In 1986 the CPB ran 38 primary schools in the area, down from 61 in 1979. The Baptist community (2,217 strong) maintain 101 churches with attached schools. The Buddhists run 135 monastic schools.

Representation in the 1985 Central Committee: Mya Thaung, the district party secretary, was elected alternate member in 1985 along with Chao Ngi Lai, the local Wa leader. Following the 1989 mutiny, Chao Ngi Lai became one of the leaders, and Mya Thaung was arrested by rebellious troops.

Troop Strength: The CPB's 12th Brigade was based in Möng Mau. Its strength is estimated at 1,000, nearly all of them are Wa. This was the unit that captured Panghsang on April 16–17, 1989.

History: The "Wild Wa" area was unadministered territory in the British time, during which the colonial presence was confined to yearly flag marches in other Wa areas. The situation remained unchanged after Burma's independence. Möng Mau and Saohpa (Pang Wei township on official Burmese maps) were the only places with any significant governmental presence. In the 1950s, large tracts of the area were taken over by Kuomintang-invaders who made alliances with local chieftains and their private armies. The CPB began penetrating the area from Kokang and China in 1969. Contacts were made with two local warlords, Chao Ngi Lai and Pao Yo Chang, who were given arms and ammunition. Saohpa was occupied in December 1969, Möng Mau on May 1, 1971, Vingngun and Loi Leün in 1972. The government forces retreated to Panglong and Hopang; the warlords joined forces with the government and became *Ka Kwe Ye* home guards. The most powerful of them, Mahasang, left for the Thai border and later set up the Wa National Army (WNA). By 1973 the entire area had come under the control of the CPB. However, the local Wa resisted the new intruders from the beginning, and the CPB was not able to subdue the population and take control of the remote areas, such as Ai Kyin, until 1974. The situation remained static from then until the mutiny, during which time government forces did not even try to penetrate the area.

The situation in 1990: Chao Ngi Lai, the local commander/civil administrator, cooperated with Pao Yo Chang in Panghsang. In April 1989, Northern Wa, Southern Wa, and Panghsang united under the banner of the Burma National United

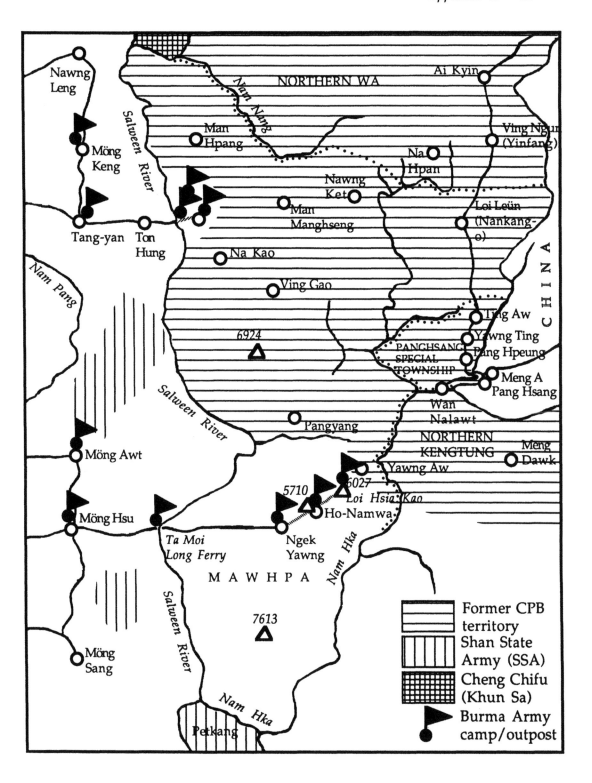

Map 7. Southern Wa District

Party/Army (မြန်မာပြည် အမျိုးသား သွေးစီးရေး ပါတီ/ တပ်မတော်) which merged with Thai-border based Wa forces in November 1989 to become the United Wa State Party/Army (UWSP/UWSA). There was also some cooperation with Kokang, but considerably less with Northern Kengtung and the Mekong River Division (815).

SOUTHERN WA DISTRICT

Area: The initial Southern Wa District comprised 6,160 square kilometers, bordered by the Salween in the west, the Chinese frontier in the east, the Nam Hka in the south and the Nam Nang in the north. The government's only toehold in the area was the garrison and the surrounding hills at Man Kang. In 1979, however, the government managed to recapture a 2,000 square kilometer area known as Mawhpa, between the Nam Hka and the Nam Nge-hpök. Panghsang also became a separate administrative unit. The present Southern Wa District therefore comprises 3,100 square kilometers. The entire area is mountainous with no valleys. The CPB divided it into five townships: Manghseng, Nawng Ket, Loi Leün, Na Kao, and Pangyang. The CPB's district headquarters was located at Vieng Kao.

Population: 53,315 in 1986 (down from 91,833 in 1979, which, however, also included about 10,000 people in Panghsang township). 39,312 were Wa; 6,613 Shan; 6,437 Lahu; 701 Chinese; 174 Mien; and 25 Kachin.

Economy and Infrastructure: The area is poor with no fertile valleys. Edible crops include hill paddy, corn, millet, and beans. There are three main cash crops: tea (1,455 viss/year), tobacco (9,269 viss/year) and opium (7,299 viss/year). The Panghsang-Möng Mau motor road passes through Loi Leün; otherwise mule tracks connect major villages. After the Min Yan Aung I operation in 1979/80, the Burmese government bulldozed a motorable road from the Salween river crossing at Ta Mot Long up to the forward position at Loi Hsia Kao. There are 25 insurgent-run primary schools in the district and a small clinic at Vieng Kao. Previously there was one clinic in each township, but the CPB closed these in the early 1980s due to lack of funds.

Representation in the 1985 Central Committee: None. There were only 2 or 3 Burman polititical officers at Vieng Kao headquarters until the 1989 mutiny.

Troop Strength: The 7th Brigade had its base near Manghseng and functioned as the buffer-security force for Panghsang. Its strength was estimated at 1,000 troops. Most of them, including the commander, were Wa, a few were Lahu or Shan.

History: Rangoon's presence was more in evidence here than in the wilder Northern Wa Hills, both during the British period and after independence. There were Burmese Army outposts at all major villages and a token governmental structure did exist. But CPB columns moved south from Northern Wa in 1972 and on June 6 the government outpost at Manghseng was overrun. Panghsang fell shortly afterwards, and by August Loi Leün and Man Hpang had been taken over as well. Mawhpa, an area inhabited mainly by Lahu, came under CPB control in 1973; the entire Southern Wa Hills except Man Kang were "liberated" by 1974. In late 1979 the government mounted a major offensive code-named Min Yan Aung I, with the aim of capturing Panghsang. The offensive fell short of that objective, but the Burmese Army managed to regain control over Mawhpa and establish a forward position at Loi Hsiao Kao, only 35 kilometers. west of Panghsang. The CPB had to retreat to the north of the Nam Nge-Hpök river. Since then there were no territorial changes despite a major offensive in the Pangyang area early 1987.

The situation in 1990: In April 1989 the district joined the Northern Wa, and Panghsang and thus came under the Burma National United Party/Army and later the United Wa State Party/Army.

PANGHSANG SPECIAL TOWNSHIP

Area: 800 square kilometers: the Panghsang valley and nearby villages in a horseshoe bend of the Nam Hka river—which forms the border with China—plus the hill country up to the Nam Pang river in the west.

Population: 7,389 Wa; 2,956 Lahu; 2,023 Shan; 487 Chinese, and 388 Mien (1987). Total: 13,243 inhabitants, not including CPB leaders and families (about 200 people) who were based in the headquarters area inside the Panghsang horseshoe.

Economy and Infrastructure: Panghsang is a prosperous, fertile valley on the Burmese side of the Nam Hka river, opposite the small town of Meng A in China. Wet paddy is widely grown in the valley and hill paddy and opium in the surrounding hills. Panghsang was also a center for the contraband trade in consumer goods from China to Burma; it has a large market with more than 100 stalls and shops as well as a video hall and several small restaurants. The CPB maintained seven primary schools in the Panghsang area with different media of instruction: Burmese, Chinese, Shan, and Lahu. The central field hospital with an operation theatre is also located at Panghsang. A printing press and a small hydroelectric power station were supplied by the Chinese in the early 1970s. Motorable dirt roads connect Panghsang with nearby villages; jeeps, trucks, and tractors are in use. A bamboo pontoon bridge leads over to Meng A on the Chinese side.

Representation in the 1985 Central Committee: Most of the CPB's Central Committee was based at Panghsang until April 1989; other members alternated between general headquarters and their respective areas. The political commissar of the Northeastern Region was Soe Thein, who was arrested by the mutineers in April 1989.

Troop Strength: Because of its secure location, Panghsang functioned as a rear base and general headquarters. The 7th Brigade in Southern Wa and the various units in Northern Kengtung provided indirect security for Panghsang. But the 851 Brigade was directly controlled by the Central Military Commission at general headquarters. Its strength was estimated at about 1,000 men, most of them Wa.

History: Panghsang was captured by the CPB after a fierce battle with government troops in June 1972. It became the headquarters of "the Northeastern War Zone" in April 1973 but was not officially proclaimed general headquarters until 1975, when the Pegu Yoma mountain stronghold in central Burma (with which the northeastern forces had failed to link up or maintain effective contact) fell to the government. In 1978 Panghsang was separated from Southern Wa District and became a "Special

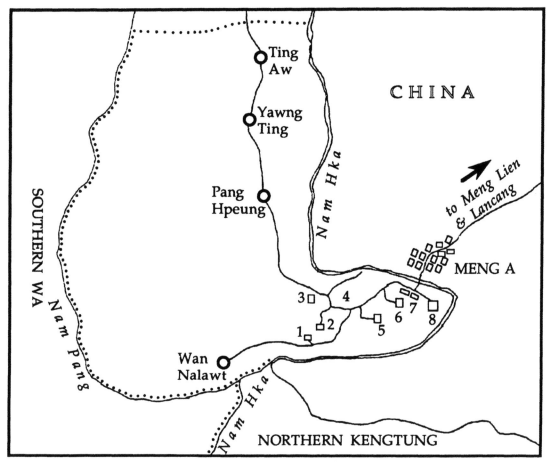

Map 8. Panghsang Special Township

1. School
2. Hospital
3. Hydroelectric power station
4. Central Market
5. Northeastern command (military headquarters)
6. Old broadcasting station
7. Armory
8. Party headquarters and leaders' houses

Township." The CPB's broadcasting station, *the People's Voice of Burma*, was located at Panghsang from 1978 to 1985, before which it was in China. In 1985 the broadcasting station was moved to the Northern Wa Hills.

The situation in 1990: Panghsang was taken over by Wa mutineers on April 17, 1989 after a brief firefight. The top CPB leaders fled to China, and the entire headquarters area is now controlled by the Wa, led by Pao Yo Chang, who is based at Panghsang, and Chao Ngi Lai, who alternates between Panghsang and Möng Mau. The Wa at Panghsang operated separately under the banner of the Burma National Democratic Party/Army and merged with other Wa forces along the Thai border in November 1989 to become the United Wa State Party/Army.

NORTHERN KENGTUNG DISTRICT

Area: 2,500 square kilometers. The CPB divided the district into six townships: Möng Pawk, Möng Pyin, Möng Kha, Möng Kwe, Man Ying, and Tsaleü. District headquarters was located at Wan Ho-tao near the Chinese border. The area is bordered by the Chinese frontier in the north, the Nam Hka in the west, and the motor road to Möng La in the east. The southern front follows a battle zone which stretches from Loi Honamtang, around the Möng Yang valley, and down to the Nam Loi river. The Möng Yang valley is itself divided by a World War I-style system of trenches and bunkers into two distinct zones: the government controls Möng Yang and the western part, while insurgents hold the big village of Hsaleü and and eastern half of the valley, and down to the Nam Loi river.

Population: 60,000 (Shan, Wa, Palaung, Lahu, Chinese, Lisu, Kachin, and half a dozen smaller ethnic groups).

Economy and Infrastructure: The area is marginally richer than other CPB areas. The valleys of Möng Pawk, Möng Pyin, and Tseleü are relatively rich in agriculture with wet paddy fields. Wan Ho-tao depends on the cross-border trade with China and is relatively prosperous. Opium poppies are widely cultivated by tribal people in the hills. Timber, mainly pinewood, is sold in large quantities to China. There is a motor road from Wan Ho-tao across the border to China and a rough mountain road from Bada in China to Hsaleü. Wide mule tracks connect other villages. A motor road (which is also a major trade route) leads from Möng Pyin down to the government-controlled garrison town of Möng Yang and on to Kengtung and Thailand. There are 23 rebel-run primary schools in the area with a total of 700 pupils.

Representation in the 1985 Central Committee: None. Two Chinese, Chen Qingyong and Xie Bing, used to be district party secretary/political commissar and vice political commissar respectively. Khun Myint, Sai Noom Pan, and Sao Khun Sa a.k.a. Michael Davies were the leaders of the 768 Brigade area but none of them ever became party members.

Troop Strength: Three CPB brigades were headquartered in this area:

6th Brigade   HQ at Wan Ho-tao. Its main area of operation is the Möng Hsat area in southern Shan State and the Thai border where it has been

Map 9. Northern Kengtung District

	cooperating with the Wa National Army (WNA). Strength: 1,000–1,500, mainly Wa.
859 Brigade	Formerly known as the 5th Brigade. HQ at Möng Pawk. It defends the southeastern flank of the Panghsang headquarters area. Strength: 1,000 (Wa, Shan, Lahu, and Chinese).
768 Brigade	A predominantly Shan brigade based in the area north and east of Möng Yang. Strength: 1,000.

History: Möng Pawn, Wan Ho-tao, and Möng Pyin were taken over during the period 1971–1973. Troops from the 815 area entered the hills around Möng Yang in 1971. After about a year, they managed to forge an alliance with Khun Myint, leader of the Shan National Army, in the hills around Möng Yang. His group was renamed the Shan People's Liberation Army in 1974. It became the 768 Brigade of the CPB in August 1976 (hence its name). Tsaleü village in the Möng Yang valley was taken over in 1976. The CPB has attacked the government garrison in Möng Yang on four occasions: in April 1973 (when it failed to capture it), November–December 1973 (when the CPB held the town for 45 days), 1981 (when it failed to capture it), and immediately after the military takeover in Rangoon in September 1988 when the CPB held the town for a few days before retreating.

The situation in 1990: The 6th Brigade continued to cooperate with the Wa forces along the Thai border. The headquarters area around Wan Ho-tao was controlled by commanders who appeared loyal to the new leaders at Panghsang. On May 15, 1989, the former 768 Brigade assumed the name used by the first Shan insurgents of the late 1950s, *Noom Suk Harn,* "the Young, Brave Warriors." Its political leader was Khun Myint and Sai Noom Pan its military commander. As noted above, Sao Khun Sa (Michael Davies) who split with the group, was assassinated in mid-May 1989. The new *Noom Suk Harn* was absorbed in late 1989 by the newly established Burma (Eastern Shan State) National Democratic Army (ပြည်ထောင်စု မြန်မာနိုင်ငံရှမ်းပြည်နယ် အရှေ့ပိုင်း အမျိုးသားဒီမိုကရေစီ တပ်မတော်). Sai Noom Pan committed suicide in April 1990.

THE MEKONG RIVER DIVISION

Area: The base area (2,732 square kilometers) is located between the Chinese border and the Nam Loi river up to the Mekong river in the east and the Möng La road in the west. A 2,400 square kilometer guerrilla zone is located south of the Nam Loi, in the hills around Möng Yawng and Möng Pa Liao. The CPB divided the area into No.1 District (Möng Hsa and Möng Khan townships in the east) and No.2 District (Möng Ma and Hsamtao townships in the west; district headquarters at Möng La), plus a Special Township around the district headquarters of Man Hpai on the Chinese border.

Population: 32,760 in the base area (11,269 in No.1 District, 13,560 in No.2 District and 7,931 in Man Hpai Special Township). 30 percent Shan (in the valleys), 30 percent Palaung (mainly in the hilly Hsamtao area), 30 percent Akha (in the eastern hills), and 10 percent Akhö (a tribe related to the Akha) and others. Approximately 20,000 people live in the guerrilla zone. Since the CPB took over the area in the early 1970s, many of its inhabitants, in particular Akha, have migrated to northern Thailand. Möng La, Möng Ma, and the villages in the the Möng Wa

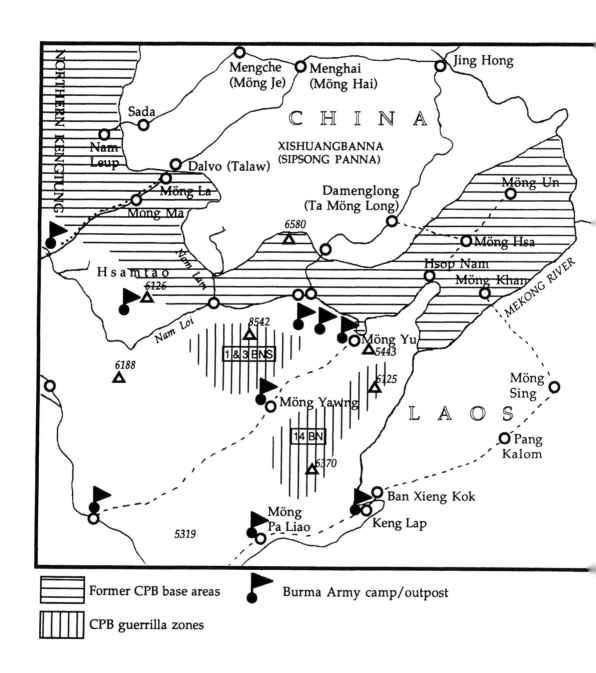

Map 10. Mekong River Division

valley form small "urban" centers in the area with large market places and solid buildings.

Economy and Infrastructure: The Möng La-Möng Ma and Möng Wa valleys are rich agricultural areas with wet paddy cultivation, coconuts, fruits, and vegetables. The hills are poor and totally dependent on opium as a cash crop. Opium is sold to refineries along the Thai-Burmese border; large quantities of timber are sold to China. Cross-border trade in Thai and Chinese consumer goods is significant; many Thai goods enter China via this area. A motor road was built in 1978–1979 from Keng Khan in the Möng Wa valley via Man Hpai to Möng Sung in China, from where the road leads on to Ta Möng Long, or Damenglong, and Jing Hong in Xishuangbanna. Another road leads from Talaw (Daluo) in China to Möng La and Möng Ma, and on to the government-controlled ferry crossing at Ta-ping on the Nam Loi river. There is only one rebel-run primary school in the area, at Möng Hsa. Most Shan villages have their own monastic schools. The CPB maintained a field hospital at Wan Hsaw near Man Hpai and a civil hospital at Möng Hsa, but many medical workers were Burmans and had to flee to China when the mutiny broke out.

Representation in the 1985 Central Committee: Tint Hlaing, the political commissar of the division, was an alternate member of the Central Committee. He was arrested by the mutineers in April 1989 but released after about a week in detention, when he left for China. The area's military commander, Lin Ming Xian (Pheung Kya-shin's son-in-law), led the local mutiny.

Troop Strength: 1,200–1,300 organized in two brigades and three independent battalions:

9th Brigade	Keng Khan and the eastern part;
11th Brigade	Möng La and the western part;
1st Battalion	the Möng Yawng guerrilla zone;
3rd Battalion	the Möng Yawng guerrilla zone;
14th Battalion	the Möng Pa Liao guerrilla zone.

In addition, there is one heavy arms battalion which does not have any designated area. Most soldiers are Akha and Shan.

History: The CPB penetrated this area in its usual way by contacting local warlords. The area was previously controlled by remnants of the Kuomintang, against whom the local Akha rebelled in 1967. The CPB intervened in 1970 and supported the Akha rebellion with arms and ammunition. Forty-two CPB cadres, led by Pe Thaung (Central Committee member since 1975) entered this area from China on October 5, 1971 and began organizing the people. The Kuomintang was driven out and retreated to the Thai border—and "the 815 War Zone" was established, named after the founding date of the CPB, August 15 (1939). The main Burmese Army camp in the area, at Möng Ma, was overrun in 1974 and Möng La was taken at about the same time. The government launched a counter-offensive, code-named Min Yan Aung II, in 1982–1983, and managed to recapture one hill in the Hsamtao area and the Pang Yu mountain (an old Kuomintang base which the CPB had taken over in 1973) south of the Möng Wa valley.

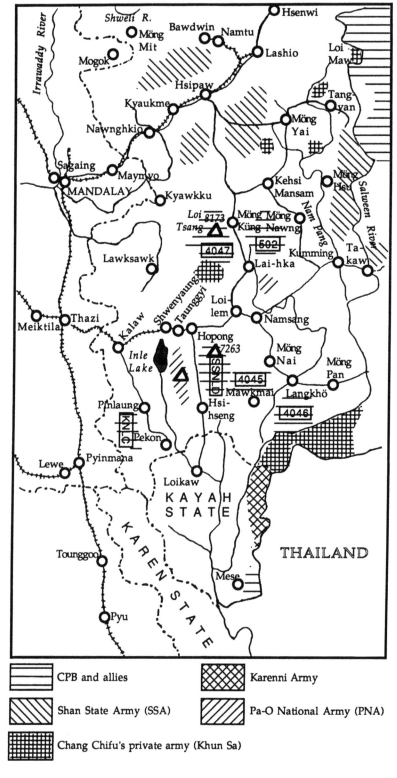

Map 11. Central Bureau Areas

The situation in 1990: This area formed an independent unit called the Burma (Eastern Shan State) National Democratic Army (ပြည်ထောင်စု မြန်မာနိုင်ငံ ရှမ်းပြည်နယ် အရှေ့ပိုင်း အမျိုးသားဒီမိုကရေစီ တပ်မတော်) led by Lin Ming Xian. He has established himself as a local warlord with his own fiefdom in the Burma-Laos-China border area. Lin Ming Xian is the son-in-law of the Kokang leader, Pheung Kya-shin.

CENTRAL BUREAU AREAS

The CPB's Central Bureau was set up in in the 1970s in central Shan State, in an attempt to create a springboard from which the northeastern base area was expected to link up with the CPB's old guerrilla zones in Burma proper. The Central Bureau areas totaled about 24,000 square kilometers and were made up of loosely defined guerrilla zones, divided into two sectors. The northern sector (north of the Taunggyi-Takaw road) comprised the CPB's former "108 War Zone" in the Kyawkku-Nawnglong-Nawng Wu area (an old stronghold which was set up in the late 1940s) and the area of operation of the former 683 Brigade. Both these units were abolished in 1980; after that, the four battalions of the old 683 Brigade—4045, 4046, 4047, and 502—were controlled directly by the Central Bureau. The main stronghold was the area near Lai-hka and Möng Küng in central Shan State, and the nearby Loi Tsang mountain range.

The southern sector (south of the Taunggyi-Takaw road) comprised regular units from the 4045 and 4046 Battalions—which operated in the Möng Nai and Wan Hat-Langkhö areas respectively—as well as three minor, allied rebel armies:

The Shan State Nationalities Liberation Organization (SSNLO), a mainly Pa-O group which is active in the Sanloi Maw mountain range southeast of Taunggyi. It is led by Tha Kalei, a Karen veteran;

The Kayan New Land Council (KNLC), a Kayan (in Burmese: Padaung) rebel army based in the hills west of Pinlaung, Pekon, and Möng Pai. Its leader is Shwe Aye a.k.a. Naing Lu Hta.

ka la la ta (ကလလတ: ကရင်နီ လူမျိုး ပေါင်းစုံ လွတ်မြောက်ရေး တပ်ဦး:), or the Karenni Nationalities Liberation Front, a pro-Communist Karenni (Kayah) group active east of Loikaw and in the Mese area opposite Thailand's Mae La Noi district, Mae Hong Son province. It is led by Nya Maung Mae.

The strength of the Central Bureau forces was as follows:

4045, 4046, 4047, and 502 Battalions:	1,400 men
+SSNLO	200 men
+KNLC	50–100 men
+*ka la la ta*	50–60 men
Total:	1,800 men

Representation in the 1985 Central Committee: Three minority cadres from the Central Bureau were elected alternate members of the new CC: Saw Ba Moe (Karen), Pao Yo Chang (Wa), and Li Ziru (Chinese). The party secretary of the Central Bureau, Mya Min, was a Burman from Pyinmana and a full member of the CC.

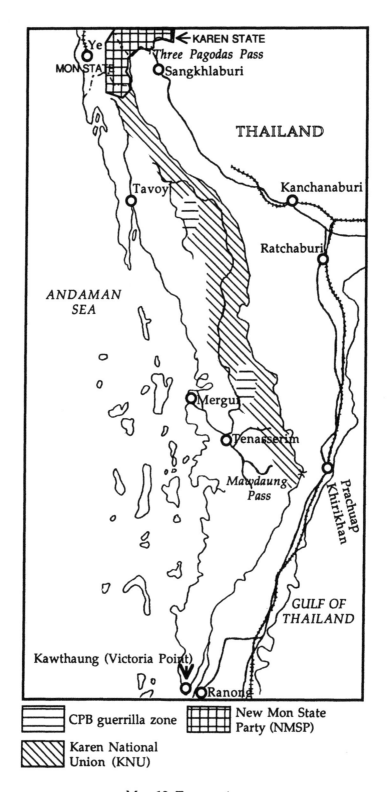

Map 12. Tenasserim

The situation in 1990: Several attempts to re-enter Burma proper via this area have failed. Cooperation with local ethnic rebel armies, mainly the Shan State Army (SSA), was deemed crucial for the success of these attempts. However, the SSA had to distance itself from the CPB in order to retain its popular support in the area, with the result that the Communists remained isolated in a few mountain ranges from which they occasionally launched ambushes on army convoys on the Taunggyi-Takaw road. On January 14, 1989 the CPB, together with the KNLC, attacked a government outpost at Taungmyint Ywathit, only 50 kms. east of Pyinmana and the Rangoon-Mandalay railway. This attack was the closest to Burma proper since 1983 when a CPB unit managed to reach Yedashe and Myhla on the railway. Most of the Central Bureau forces are Shan, Wa, Pa-O, Kayan (Padaung), and Karenni (Kayah). Following the 1989 mutiny, two of its top military commanders—Pao Yo Chang and Li Ziru—have been based at Panghsang. The rank-and-file is reported to be loyal to the new, non-Communist leadership.

TENASSERIM

The Tavoy-Mergui region of Tenasserim Division is an old CPB stronghold; Thakin Ba Thein Tin was born in Tavoy in 1914 and led the resistance there against the Japanese during World War II. In the late 1940s strongholds were established in the mountainous jungle region in Tayetchaung, Launglong, Tavoy, and Thaungbaing townships in Tavoy district; near the towns of Palaw, Tenasserim; and the area immediately east of Mergui. But the CPB forces in Tenasserim had almost no contact with the northeastern base area until the Third Party Congress in 1985 when the local party secretary, Saw Han, secretly went to Panghsang. Two other leaders of the Tenasserim unit, Soe Lwin and Aye Hla, were also elected to the Central Committee at that time although they did not attend the congress. The 1989 mutiny did not affect Tenasserim: a few hundred CPB guerrillas are still holding out in small pockets east of Tavoy and Mergui, and they maintain a small camp opposite Thailand's Kachanaburi province.

ARAKAN STATE

The Arakan area near the Bangladesh border is one of the CPB's oldest strongholds, since the first party unit there was set up in Sandoway in 1939. The Arakanese Communists went underground along with the rest of the party in March 1948. Other insurgent groups were also active in the Arakan Yoma, notably rival "Red Flag" Communists, Muslim rebels in Maungdaw and Buthidaung, and smaller Arakanese nationalist groups. A separate Communist Party of Arakan was set up in 1956. The CPB, however, remained the main rebel group in Arakan, with more than 1,000 troops and strongholds in the area between the Hsaitin and Kaladan rivers and around the towns of Myohaung, Minbya, Kyauktaw, and An. The Arakan unit of the CPB had only limited contact with the rest of the CPB, but in 1979 the local leader, Kyaw Mya, left for Panghsang and the northeastern base area via Bangladesh and China. He was succeeded by Ye Tun, who surrendered during the 1980 amnesty along with most of the remaining troops. In 1990, the CPB still had a few hundred activists in the area near the Bangladesh border, only a handful of them armed.

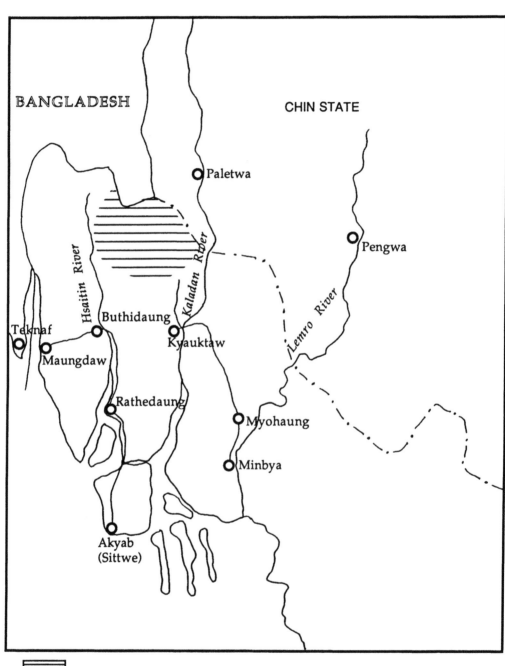

Map 13. Arakan State

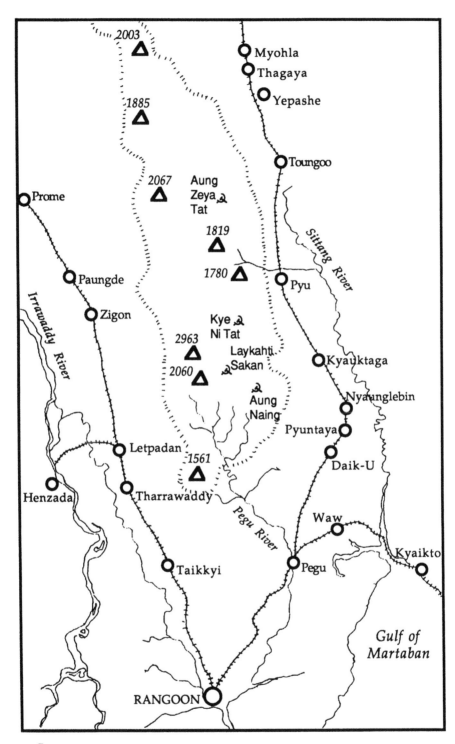

☭ CPB camps in the early 1970s

Map 14. The Pegu Yoma

OLD AREAS

Immediately after the outbreak of the civil war on March 28, 1948, the CPB established strongholds in a number of areas in central Burma, the Irrawaddy Delta, the Arakan region, and in Tenasserim. A few of these old strongholds remained in CPB hands until the 1970s:

Pegu Yoma, the wide, forested mountain area just north of Rangoon, became a CPB base area in the early 1950s and the site of its headquarters in 1959. The first party chairman, Thakin Than Tun, was killed there by a government infiltrator on September 8, 1968, and on March 15, 1975, government forces killed his successor, Thakin Zin, and party secretary Thakin Chit. Shortly afterwards the last remaining CPB troops withdrew from the Pegu Yoma, and the civilian population was resettled by the government in other areas in central Burma. Most of the mountain range has been uninhabited since 1975. The CPB made a few unsuccessful attempts to re-enter Pegu Yoma in the late 1970s and in 1983.

The Pokaung Range on the border between Arakan State and Magwe Division, west of Minbu and Thayetmyo, was a CPB stronghold until its commander, Thet Tun, surrendered during the 1980 amnesty.

The Irrawaddy Delta region was a stronghold which the CPB shared with Karen rebels. Successive government offensives during the period 1966–1971 forced the CPB, as well as the Karen rebels, to retreat to the Pegu Yoma. The CPB's main stronghold in the delta was located at Lemyethna in the west.

The Pinlebu area in northern Sagaing Division remained a CPB stronghold until 1970–1971. CPB units operated over an area stretching from the Chindwin river to Katha, on the border with Kachin State. When the northeastern base area was established, the CPB on two occasions tried to re-enter the countryside around Pinlebu. One unit, led by Bo Kyaw Moe, code-named Force 180, crossed the Irrawaddy river in March 1981 and managed to reach the countryside north of Pinlebu. But Bo Kyaw Moe and most of his men were killed by government forces; only a few survivors managed to make it back to the northeast. A second unit, Force 102, tried to enter the Pinlebu from Kachin State in February 1983, but failed. Only about 18 men ventured further down Sagaing Division, where they were chased by government troops and had to retreat westwards across the Chindwin into the Naga Hills. They eventually returned to the northeast in 1985.

Appendix III:
Ethnic Insurgent Groups in Burma

Since shortly after Burma achieved independence in 1948, an abundance of ethnic rebel armies have been fighting for autonomy and, in some cases, even for secession from the union. Some of these rebel groups are little more than local warlord armies; others have genuine political goals with varying degrees of broad-based popular support. In 1976, the more politically oriented groups united under the common banner of the National Democratic Front (NDF). In 1989 the NDF had eleven members, divided into three commands for regional cooperation.

NORTHERN COMMAND:

The Kachin Independence Organization/Army (KIO/KIA) with 8,000–10,000 troops is by far the largest and best organized non-Communist rebel army in Burma. It operates over a 40,000 square kilometer area in Kachin State and the Kachin-inhabited hills of northeastern Shan State. The KIO chairman, Brang Seng, left Kachin State in 1986 and reached Thailand six months later. Since then he has traveled extensively in Asia and Europe to propagate the NDF cause: a political solution to the civil war and regional autonomy for Burma's national minorities. In his absence a committee led by the KIO's vice chairman, Major-General Zau Mai (who is also the chief of staff of the KIA), has handled day-to-day affairs in Kachin State.

The Shan State Progress Party/the Shan State Army (SSPP/SSA) is the main rebel group among the Shans. It has, however, suffered several splits, defections, and internal rivalries over the past ten years. Consequently its strength has gone down from a peak of 5,000–6,000 in the late 1970s to about 2,500–3,000 in 1989. In that year the SSPP/SSA split and the bulk of the fighting force, led by Hso Hten, reached an agreement with the Burmese Army, similar to that of the former CPB forces. The remnants, led by Col. Sai Lek, are closely allied with the KIO/KIA. Unlike the KIO/KIA, the SSPP/SSA does not have any secure base areas; it operates in a large guerrilla zone west of the Salween river, from Namhsan in the north down to the Thai border.

The Palaung State Liberation Party/Army (PSLP/PSLA) has about 500–600 troops and operates in the Palaung-inhabited hills of northern Shan State, south of the Shweli river. Its leader, Ai Mong, is also a close ally of the KIO/KIA.

The Chin National Front/Army (CNF/CNA) joined the NDF in early 1989. The CNF was set up in 1985, but it was not until November 14, 1988 that it formed a military wing, the CNA. John Khaw Kim Thang is the chairman of the CNF. In 1989 a few hundred Chin guerrillas were undergoing training provided by the KIA in Kachin State. Until the formation of the CNA, Chin State was the only minority area in Burma which did not have its own rebel army.

CENTRAL COMMAND:

The Wa National Organization/Army (WNO/WNA), was led by Mahasang, a former Wa chieftain from Vingngun, who played an important role in encouraging the Wa soldiers in the CPB to rise up against the old leadership. The WNA had nearly 1,000 troops based along the Thai border. In November 1989, most of these joined the Wa segment of the former CPB to become the United Wa State Party/Army. Until the 1989 mutiny, the WNO/WNA was based solely along the Thai border and had no presence in the Wa Hills. While several UWSP/UWSA leaders are involved in the Golden Triangle opium trade, some of the younger cadres are more politically motivated.

The Pa-O National Organization/Army (PNO/PNA) has about 500–600 men who operate in the Pa-O–inhabited hills southeast of the Shan State capital of Taunggyi. It is led by Aung Kham Hti, a former Buddhist monk from Taunggyi. There has been little fighting between the PNA and government forces and the two appear to have some kind of understanding, probably to counter the influence of the CPB-affiliated, "Red Pa-O" organization, the SSNLO. Following the mutiny, the situation became unclear; attempts were made to unify the two rival Pa-O organizations but with limited success.

The Karenni National Progressive Party/the Karenni Army (KNPP/KA) was quite strong in the mid-1970s, but its strength has dwindled to less than 500 following factional infighting and desertions. It operates in Kayah State, between the Salween river and the Thai border. The KNPP is led by Bya Reh and the KA by Brigadier-General Bee Htoo.

The Lahu National Organization/Army (LNO/LNA) is a small group, led by Kya U, who has only a handful of soldiers under his command. Kya U previously led a Lahu rebel army based at Doi Lang on the Thai border. He surrendered in 1983, but went underground again about a year later to set up the LNO/LNA.

SOUTHERN COMMAND:

The Karen National Union/the Karen National Liberation Army (KNU/KNLA) is led by General Bo Mya. Its bases along the Thai border came under fierce attack by government troops in early 1984. During the first months of 1989, the government forces eventually overran a number of these bases after besieging them for five years: Klerday, Mae La, Maw Pokay, and Wangkha. This was made possible by the improved Thai-Burmese relations which followed a visit to Rangoon in December by acting Thai supreme commander, General Chaovalit Yongchaiyuth. Intelligence reports indicated that the Burmese Army were allowed to use Thai territory to capture these bases along the Moei border river. Casualties have not been heavy on the KNLA's side, but many privates have deserted to Thailand and settled in Karen villages there. The strength of the KNLA was estimated at 3,500–4,000 in 1989.

The New Mon State Party/the Mon National Liberation Army (NMSP/MNLA) was rather weak until the Burmese Army launched the campaign against the Karen rebels along the Moei river. As a direct result of that fighting, most of the illicit border trade between Burma and Thailand moved southwards from the Karen-controlled border crossings to Three Pagodas Pass, where the Mon rebels operate. This enabled the MNLA to collect more tax and to increase its strength from less than 1,000 to more than 2,000 today. In July 1988, however, Karen rebel troops attacked the Mon at Three Pagodas Pass in an attempt to wrest control over the lucrative border trade from them. The fighting lasted for more than a month with heavy casualties on both sides. A ceasefire agreement was reached in late 1988 and the border gate was reopened in 1989. The NMSP chairman, Nai Shwe Kyin, is a veteran of the anti-Rangoon ethnic resistance in Burma. His deputy, Nai Nol Lar, died at Three Pagodas Pass on August 8, 1989 while giving a speech to dissident students along the Thai-Burmese border.

The National United Front of Arakan (NUFA) has less than 100 soldiers, most of whom are based in the KNU area along the Thai border; only a handful are in Arakan State. Its leader, Khaing Ye Khaing, is believed to be somewhere in the India-Bangladesh-Burma border region. In October 1989, the Arakan Liberation Party, the Arakan Independence Organization, the Tribal National Party, and the Communist Party of Arakan merged under the NUFA banner.

In November 1988, the NDF, together with a number of ethnic Burman anti-government groups, set up the Democratic Alliance of Burma (DAB) in an attempt to broaden the armed resistance against the military regime in Rangoon. But of these groups only the Committee for Restoration of Democracy in Burma (CRDB) and the All-Burma Students' Democratic Front (ABSDF) are of any significance. The CRDB is a US-based organization of Burmese exiles; the ABSDF is an umbrella organization of Burmese students who fled to the Thai border after the military crackdown on dissent in September 1988. A few hundred ABSDF members have undergone military training in areas controlled by Karen and Mon rebels, but neither group has been able to arm and equip the students. Only in Kachin State is there a full battalion of students who have been trained and armed by the KIA.

OTHER ETHNIC REBEL ARMIES:

Naga: the National Socialist Council of Nagaland (NSCN), a group led by Naga from India, maintained a base area in the Burmese Naga Hills of northern Sagaing Division from the early 1970s until 1988. It was led by Isak Chishi Swu and Thuingaleng Muivah, both Naga from India, and S.S. Khaplang, a Burmese Naga. In 1988 Burmese Naga led by Khaplang drove the Indian Naga out of their base area northwest of Singkaling Hkamti and established links with the Kachin rebels. Khaplang has 400–500 men under his command. Some NSCN remnants, led by Muivah, were operating in the Somra area opposite Manipur in late 1989. Another Naga faction, the Naga National Council (NNC), maintains a small base area in Sagaing Division. It has about 160 armed men.

Arakan: There are a number of small rebel groups in Arakan State, but none of them is of any significance. Apart from the NUFA, CPB remnants in Arakan maintain camps along the Bangladesh border, as does a small unit of the otherwise largely defunct Communist Party (Red Flag). The Muslim minority in Maungdaw and Buthidaung townships has several rebel groups, the main one being the Arakan Rohingya Islamic Front (ARIF), led by Shabbir Hussain.

Warlord armies: the main private army in Burma is the Tai Revolutionary Council (TRC) with its Möng Tai Army (MTA). It was formed in 1986 when the Shan United Revolutionary Army (SURA) of Moh Heng and the Shan United Army (SUA) of drug kingpin Chang Chifu, alias Khun Sa, joined forces. Despite its name, the TRC/MTA should not be regarded as a rebel army; its main preoccupation is drug smuggling and the protection of heroin refineries along the Thai-Burmese border. It has about 2,500–3,000 heavily armed troops who move over a fairly large area in southern Shan State, as well as the Tang-yan/Loi Maw area in northern Shan State. Official reports from both the Burmese and Thai governments claiming that they are "cracking down" on Khun Sa should be treated with a great deal of skepticism. While the Burmese Army has launched major offensives against all ethnic rebel armies in the country, it has always left Khun Sa alone. Kickbacks from the traffic constitute an important source of income for many army officers, and Khun Sa provides the Burmese military with intelligence information on the movements of insurgents in Shan State. He is similarly well connected to high-ranking military officers in Thailand.

ABBREVIATIONS

ABPO	the All-Burma Peasants' Organization. Socialist-dominated peasants' organization in the 1940s and early 1950s.
ABPU	the All-Burma Peasants' Union. Communist-sponsored peasants' organization in the late 1940s.
ABSU	the All-Burma Students' Union. AFPFL-affiliated students' union active in the 1940s and the 1950s.
ABTUC	the All-Burma Trade Union Congress. Set up in 1945 by Thakin Ba Hein. Pro-Communist.
AFPFL	the Anti-Fascist People's Freedom League; the most important political party in Burma in the late 1940s and in the 1950s.
BIA	the Burma Independence Army. Founded by Aung San in 1941.
BDA	the Burma Defense Army (succeeded the BIA in 1942).
BNA	the Burma National Army (succeeded the BDA in 1943).
BNDAA	the Burma National Democratic Alliance Army. Set up by CPB mutineers in Kokang District in March 1989.
BNUP	the Burma National United Party. Set up by CPB mutineers at Panghsang in April 1989. Renamed the United Wa State Party/Army in November.
BSP	the Burma Socialist Party. Political party in Burma in the 1940s and the 1950s.
BSPP	the Burma Socialist Program Party. The ruling party in Burma from 1962 to 1988.
BWPP	the Burma Workers' and Peasants' Party. The main legal leftist party in Burma in the 1950s.
CPA	the Communist Party of Arakan. Local Communist party in Arakan State, not affiliated with the CPB.
CPB	the Communist Party of Burma. Founded in 1939, defunct in 1989. Incorrectly referred to as "the Burma Communist Party" by the government in Rangoon.
CPC	the Communist Party of China.
CPI	the Communist Party of India.

CPM	the Communist Party of Malaya.
CP (RF)	the Communist Party (Red Flag). Set up in 1946 when Thakin Soe broke away from the main CPB. Defunct in 1970 when Thakin Soe was captured by government forces.
CPT	the Communist Party of Thailand.
KIA	the Kachin Independence Army. An ethnic Kachin rebel army, set up in 1961.
KNLC	the Kayan New Land Council. A CPB-affiliated Kayan (Padaung) ethnic rebel army in Shan State.
KNU	the Karen National Union. An ethnic Karen rebel organization. Went underground in 1949.
NDF	the National Democratic Front. An umbrella organization of about a dozen non-Communist ethnic rebel armies in Burma. Set up in 1976.
NUF	the National Unity Front. A legal leftist front (centered around the BWPP) active in the 1950s.
PBF	the Patriotic Burmese Forces (succeeded the BNA in 1945).
PCP	the People's Comrade Party. Set up when the PVO split in 1948. In rebellion until 1957, when the entire party surrendered and was legalized.
PLAB	the People's Liberation Army of Burma. The CPB's first army. Merged with the RBA in 1950 to become the People's Army.
PLF	the People's Liberation Front. Set up in 1989 (formerly the CPB's 101 War Zone in Kachin State).
PRP	the People's Revolutionary Party. Political party in Burma in the 1940s. Became the BSP in 1945.
PVO	the People's Volunteer Organization. Paramilitary organization set up after World War II. One faction went into rebellion in 1948 and became the PCP.
RBA	the Revolutionary Burma Army. Formed by mutineers from the regular Burma Army in 1948. Merged with the CPB's forces in 1950.
RUSU	the Rangoon University Students' Union. Founded in 1931, crushed after the 1962 coup and revived in 1988.
SLORC	State Law and Order Restoration Council.
SSA	the Shan State Army. An ethnic Shan rebel army set up in 1964.
SSNLO	the Shan State Nationalities Liberation Organization. A CPB-affiliated ethnic Pa-O rebel army in Shan State.
TUC(B)	the Trade Union Congress (Burma). BSP-affiliated trade union organization in the late 1940s and early 1950s.

UWSP/UWSA   the United Wa State Party/Army. Set up on November 3, 1989, uniting the former BNUP and non-Communist Wa forces along the Thai border.

WNA   the Wa National Army. An ethnic Wa rebel army in Shan State set up in 1973. Most of the rank and file joined the new United Wa State Army in November 1989.

www.ingramcontent.com/pod-product-compliance
Ingram Content Group UK Ltd.
Pitfield, Milton Keynes, MK11 3LW, UK
UKHW052120180325
456429UK00005B/75

9 780877 271239